Out Of The Darkness
UFO Revelations And The Arrival Of the Mysterious Planet X

By Commander X

With Additional Material By:

Timothy Green Beckley

Poke Runyon

Tim R. Swartz

Inner Light/Global Communications

Out Of The Darkness
UFO Revelations And The Arrival Of the Mysterious Planet X

Commander X

Copyright © 2014 – Timothy Green Beckley
DBA Global Communications, All Rights Reserved

Nonfiction – Paranormal/Mythology/Astronomy

No part of this book may be reproduced, stored in retrieval system or transmitted in any form or by any means, electronic, mechanical, photocopying, recording, without express permission of the publisher.

Timothy Green Beckley: Editorial Director
Carol Rodriguez: Publishers Assistant
Sean Casteel: Associate Editor
William Kern: Editorial Assistant
Author: Commander X
Cover Art: Tim R. Swartz

Printed in the United States of America

For free catalog write:
Global Communications
P.O. Box 753
New Brunswick, NJ 08903

Free Subscription to Conspiracy Journal E-Mail Newsletter
www.conspiracyjournal.com

PSYCHIC AND UFO REVELATIONS – 5
By Timothy Green Beckley

CHAPTER ONE: Out of the Darkness – 13

CHAPTER TWO: What Is Planet X? – 28

CHAPTER THREE: The Mayan Calendar – 32

CHAPTER FOUR: The Planet X/Nibiru Controversy – 54

CHAPTER FIVE: The Suppression of Immanuel Velikovsky – 71

CHAPTER SIX: Prophets and Prophecies – 81

CHAPTER SEVEN: The New Dawn of Consciousness – 109

CHAPTER EIGHT: How To Survive The Changing Times – 116

CHAPTER NINE: An E-Mail From A Norwegian Politician – 129

CHAPTER TEN: The Fallen Angel Samyaza's Prophecy of Doom – 139

POLAR SHIFT AND THE DROWNING OF AMERICA - 147

Out Of The Darkness – UFO Revelations And Planet X

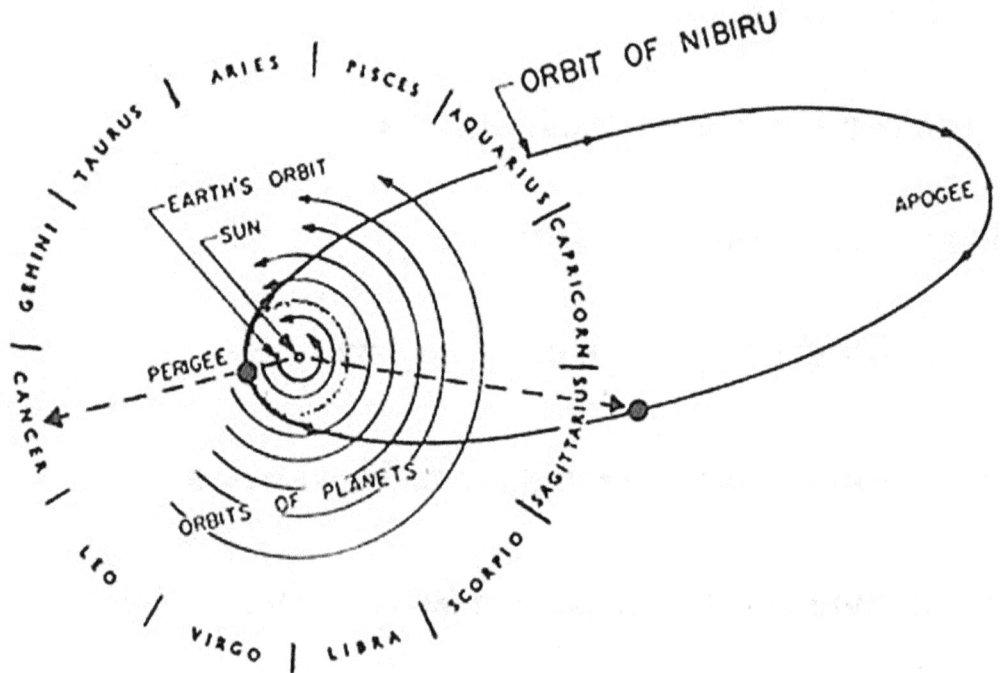

Something out there beyond the furthest reaches of the known solar system is tugging at Uranus and Neptune. A gravitational force keeps perturbing the two giant planets, causing irregularities in their orbits. The force suggests a presence far away and unseen, a large object, the long-sought Planet X. Astronomers are so certain of this planet's existence that they have already named it "Planet X."

PSYCHIC AND UFO REVELATIONS
By Timothy Green Beckley

ACCORDING to those who claim to be "experts" on the subject, Planet X may come at any time, or it might not come at all (my trend of thinking). However, just about everyone we have spoken to over the course of the last three or four decades (yes, we are as old as the hills) have maintained that our planet is in for some drastic earth changes.

Though 2012 has come and gone and there are no Maya in our neighborhood that we know of, certainly things have become to "slide" as far as weather patterns and global chaos go. So I don't think we are out of the woods.

Thus this pungent, up to date, presentation on the "dark side" of things. Hopefully, what we have seen around us will not be a longstanding trend. We are keeping our cosmic fingers crossed that an upgrading of our current circumstances may be due – hopefully with the help of some friendly beings from other worlds, other realms or the future.

Spaceship 54 where are you???

It is not our purpose to validate psychic phenomena or even such simple matters as the reality of extrasensory perception. Most of those "open-minded" enough to purchase such a book as this must already be familiar with the valuable research done by investigators such as the late Prof. J.B. Rhine of Duke University.

Taking into consideration the fact that UFO pilots and crew members must be "light years" beyond where we stand on the evolutionary scale, it stands to reason that their psychic abilities would have progressed to the point where they are able to accomplish almost any feat.

Out Of The Darkness – UFO Revelations And Planet X

Situated in various countries around the world are highly sensitive earthlings who are able to "tune in" to the wavelengths of these alien beings and actually act as sort of a "radio receiver" in picking up messages that are being "beamed" from beyond our atmosphere. Some of this information is taken down in the form of automatic writing, but usually the man or woman actually allows his vocal cords to be taken over so that there is no chance for human error or misinterpretation.

The majority of the "sermons" which have been delivered through these "Channels," as they are often referred to, deal with upcoming events and trends on Earth, primarily geological, meteorological and political. What makes it quite obvious that no fraud is being committed by these "Channels" is the fact that the messages are all similar even though they are "beamed" to vastly separate parts of the world.

Also beyond mere coincidence is the astounding fact that the extraterrestrials who are extending their hand in friendship almost always have the same names. Names that keep cropping up over and over again in such communications include Monka, Mohada, Deska, and most popular of all, Ashtar.

It is repeatedly stated that Ashtar is in charge of thousands of space ships as well as the "Commander of ten million space men, now occupying bases established within range of your planet." Some of the beings who are making themselves heard are supposedly human just as we are – flesh and blood creatures – while others have rid themselves of their physical bodies and now exist in a sort of computerized form.

These entities of vast knowledge are said to travel from solar system to solar system in huge "Mother Ships" but sometimes they actually take up residence on other planets which orbit around our sun. For according to these channels, believe it or not, there is supposedly intelligent life on Venus, Mars, Jupiter, Saturn and so forth – this despite what astronomers and other scientists might have to say.

Though some of this life may be in the solid form such as we humans, many of these beings are said to exist on higher levels of vibration and in other dimensions which are normally invisible to the human eye. We will not try to sway your beliefs. We simply ask that you read the information that is being passed along and judge for yourself its validity. We ask nothing but your attention and a promise that you will study this material carefully for your own benefit, and not for ours.

Out Of The Darkness – UFO Revelations And Planet X

WHY THEY COME AND WHAT IT IS THEY WANT

"They do not wish to cause us any harm. They don't care to be recognized or hassled by people, and so they frequently share helpful information through mental telepathy," acknowledges one who is highly thought of in her community, having assisted families and law officers in over 50 crime-related cases.

The psychic says that aliens are working in hospitals, as well as energy-related fields, space technology and in various jobs related to science. Their characteristics include being very efficient, above average in intelligence, easy to get along with, and they never ask questions except about their duties.

They look like Earth people and include the entire spectrum of race characteristics and color. They dress simply, with very little jewelry except a watch. They need little sleep and they always seem to be in excellent health.

Sometimes they have brown markings on their hands and arms that form star patterns. Their purpose is to study Earth in order to gain knowledge that will be helpful to the entire universe. For instance, the people of Earth have many illnesses that are caused by the pollution of air and water. Most of Earth's problems are not experienced on other planets – they can prevent them from happening by studying our mistakes.

THE BATTLE FOR MAN'S MIND

Some time ago, Wilbur Smith figured out that Earth was more or less a "battleground." The Canadian scientist, and Channel for information from space, saw our globe as being pulled upon in a cosmic "tug-of-war" between the forces of good and evil. He saw this conflict – taking place in this dimension as well as on other planes – coming to a final conclusion sometime in the near future.

"I propose," declared Smith, "to give a warning of grave danger which we are all, consciously or unconsciously, facing in a world in which two great forces are striving to gain control of man's mind. This struggle has been going on from time immemorial, but never in the world's history has the conflict been more intense than it is in this present era of confusion and unrest. In the old days, mankind was often made to suffer physically from unspeakable things in the name of power, but today, with man's mind more developed and better educated, he is now facing the prospect of a refinement of even greater mental and spiritual cruelty – unless he is prepared to protect himself with right thinking. The two great forces involved in trying to influence man's thinking may be described as positive, i.e., thoughts in harmony with the concept of a love of God and the brotherhood of man, and negative, those encompassing anti-Christ motives designed to gain control over man for the purpose of power. This battle for Man's mind is being waged on two fronts, the physical and the metaphysical, and the object of the fight is to bring about either the spiritual salvation or destruction of homo sapiens."

Apparently, Smith determined that UFOs were most important in Earth's overall spiritual development, especially as they relate to the End Times.

"We may summarize the entire flying saucer picture as follows: We have arrived at a time in our development when we must make a final choice between right and wrong. The people from elsewhere are much concerned about the choice which we will make, partly because it will have its repercussions on them and partly because we are their blood brothers and they are truly concerned with our welfare. There is a cosmic law against interfering in the affairs of others, so they are not allowed to help us directly even though they could easily do so. We must make our own choice of our own free will. Present trends indicate a series of events which may require the help of these people and they stand by ready and willing to render that help. In fact, they have already helped us a great deal, along lines which do not interfere with our freedom of choice. In time, when certain events have transpired, and we are so oriented that we can accept these people from elsewhere, they will meet us freely on the common ground of mutual understanding and trust, and we will be able to learn from them and bring about the Golden Age all men everywhere desire deep within their hearts."

A true New Age visionary, Smith fully realized that "which is hidden from view" often is as important as that which we can see with our eyes. Thus he turned his thoughts to other planes and realms in order to more fully understand that which is at play in the universe as concerns our way of life in the years just ahead.

"Messages received through esoteric sources, purporting to come from Space Brothers who take an active interest in the spiritual welfare of the inhabitants of our planet, warn us that an even greater conflict is being fought on the metaphysical plane where intelligent beings of both a higher and a lower spiritual order than themselves are waging a fierce battle for Man's mind. The lower or negative forces, damned themselves by wrong thinking, are projecting strong thoughts Earthward in an attempt to bring about our spiritual downfall. On the other hand, Space Brothers and other spiritual guardians of our planet are concentrating equally hard on sending out positive thoughts of goodwill and brotherly love. Thus we are being bombarded from the metaphysical plane by two conflicting schools of thought, and, free will being the criterion of spiritual advancement, it is left to us which we choose to accept. However, from a purely local point of view, if we want to save ourselves a lot of sorrow both in this life and lives to come, we should arm ourselves mentally against the onslaught of negative thoughts.

"This is no time for confused or apathetic thinking – often the future breeding-ground of negative thoughts. Nor should we be just receivers and disseminators of the thoughts we pick up. Rather, we should get on the transmitting end and constantly project positive thoughts of goodwill to all. Every positive thought neutralizes a negative thought, so we shall be serving not only ourselves but all humanity.

"In the final analysis, there are two simple, clear-cut maxims to be observed for complete protection from the negative forces at work on this planet: (1) Acknowledgement and love of God as the Father of all Creation, and...(2) Brotherly love extended to all His creatures throughout the universe.

"Anything else which interferes with these two beliefs should be vigorously rejected. Further, if we return love for hate, hate will die of malnutrition, for it can only feed on returned hatred. Let us rather pray for spiritual enlightenment for these wretched souls who seek to harm us.

"In conclusion, if any of you have doubts about the veracity of the telepathic and inspirational messages received from Space Brothers and others interested in the welfare of our planet, just ask yourselves this one vital question – 'Are these messages good and true and for the benefit of mankind on Earth?' If, as you surely must, you come up with an answer of 'Yes,' then it is obvious that it is the hand of God at work, no matter what medium He chooses to use."

TIME FOR CHANGE

Dr. Wendy M. Lockwood of Sedalia, Colorado, a student of metaphysics who holds a doctor's degree from the Brotherhood of the White Temple, says that the entire Cosmos is nearing its material end, and that all intelligences from all dimensions, interlocking spaces and planets must at this time establish enduring harmony with one another.

Dr. Lockwood believes that we are presently 23 years into the Age of Aquarius, and that the so-called "Aliens of Light" are working very vigorously to bring Earth into perfect rapport with the rest of the universe. Dr. Lockwood maintains that included among the goals of the UFOnauts are the following principles:

1. Join earthmen as one of them.

2. Counsel and train man in higher ways.

3. Aid the peace-makers whenever danger threatens them.

4. Help prepare Earth for the great trials soon to besiege this planet.

5. Aid man in evolving peace and technology.

6. Reveal high-secret knowledge to those who qualify through virtue.

7. Act as a bridge between obsolete beliefs and superstitions to greater and true teachings and systems.

8. Help establish Universal Brotherhood, total acceptance and understanding of all species, regardless of form or culture.

9. Aid man in re-awakening his 6th sense, the sense which acts as his preserver of harmony and peace.

10. Teach the secrets of immortality and eternal youth.

11. Teach man how to manipulate the fixed Universe Laws.

Dr. Lockwood is convinced that the main reason we are being visited at this time is due to the fact that the UFOnauts are "helping to prepare man for the last great catastrophe. It's very near now," she states, "possibly within the next 5o years. There may be a devastating global war or vast, worldwide earthquakes, or an event caused by the gravitational pull of a currently unknown celestial object."

Others who have studied all the available information feel pretty much the same way. For example, Laura Mundo, who runs the Flying Saucer Information Center in Inkster, Michigan, believes that alien beings are trying to help us to help ourselves "before the atmosphere becomes unbearable due to increased sunspot activity, which is creating extremes in weather, people's actions, natural catastrophes as well as causing confusion in many other psychics, UFO contactees and New Age channels we have conversed with." Laura is of the opinion that the UFOnauts are "here to help us through a period of great crisis."

Out Of The Darkness – UFO Revelations And Planet X

"Those who qualify," she states, "will be taken to a place of safety in the space people's insulated ships, through the unbelievable planetary turmoil, and come back after the sunspots settle down."

Laura says that as far back as 1955 she received a message on her shortwave radio from a spaceman telling her that time was short for mankind. She is convinced this message is coming true today. Almost every clairvoyant we have communicated with agrees that these changes are going to happen though they insist there is no way of telling how extreme they will be. There are even some who insist the planet will become uninhabitable for years to come because of an axis shift which will send our planet into another orbit and change the climates on the planet.

The late archaeologist and UFOlogist, Dr. George Hunt Williamson, summed it up eloquently when he said: "Many so-called prophets today are foretelling horrible destruction and doom for the people of Earth. They claim life is eternal, yet they fear the transition called 'death.' The space friends are here to help us, not to destroy us . . . and although there are going to be vast changes taking place from time to time on the physical, mental and spiritual planes, still only the good is to be inherited by man on this sorrowful planet!

"Earthman has reached the stage in his evolution where he must be shown that he is not merely a lonely accident on one world only. His brothers and sisters exist on literally billions and billions of worlds in the Omniverse! As we come more and more under the beneficent rays of Aquarius, cosmic-ray bombardment will become more intensified and EVERYTHING on our planet will be changed vibrationally.

"For centuries, Theology has battled Science, and vice versa. What they are arguing about is not known, for the two are really one, and will become one in the 'Golden Dawn' approaching rapidly. All former theories will be discarded . . . or at least improved upon. We will know definitely where we have been inaccurate in the past and why! Truth will not contradict Truth. Therefore our Philosophy of Life will be built on a science that recognizes a Creator of the Cosmos and a Divine Plan working everywhere!

"No longer will we be required to follow certain ritualistic practices or believe certain dogmas in order to get into 'heaven.' On the other hand, we will no longer have to swing to the other side of the road to embrace the cold, bare facts of materialistic science. In short, we are about to 'level off' or 'get in balance.'"

Out Of The Darkness – UFO Revelations And Planet X

Art By Carol Rodriguez

CHAPTER ONE
Out of the Darkness

On March 1, 2008 scientists at Kobe University in western Japan announced that they believe another planet up to two-thirds the size of the Earth was orbiting in the far reaches of the solar system. The researchers said calculations using computer simulations led them to conclude it was only a matter of time before the mysterious "Planet X" was found.

"Because of the very cold temperature, its surface would be covered with ice, icy ammonia and methane," Kobe University professor Tadashi Mukai, the lead researcher, told reporters. "The possibility is high that a yet unknown, planet-class celestial body, measuring 30 percent to 70 percent of the Earth's mass, exists in the outer edges of the solar system." "If research is conducted on a wide scale, the planet is likely to be discovered in less than 10 years," it said.

Planet X – so called by scientists as it is yet undiscovered – would have an oblong elliptical solar orbit and circle the sun every thousand years, the team said, estimating its radius was 17 to 30 billion miles. The study comes two years after school textbooks had to be rewritten when Pluto was booted out of the list of planets.

Pluto was discovered by the American astronomer Clyde Tombaugh in 1930 in the so-called Kuiper belt, a chain of icy debris in the outer reaches of the solar system. In 2006, nearly a decade after Tombaugh's death, the International Astronomical Union ruled the celestial body was merely a dwarf planet in the cluttered Kuiper belt.

The astronomers said Pluto's oblong orbit overlapped with that of Neptune, excluding it from being a planet. It defined the solar system as consisting solely of the classical set of Mercury, Venus, Earth, Mars, Jupiter, Saturn, Uranus and Neptune. The team noted that more than 1,100 celestial bodies have been found in the outer reaches of the solar system since the mid-1990s.

Out Of The Darkness – UFO Revelations And Planet X

"But it would be the first time to discover a celestial body of this size, which is much larger than Pluto," Mukai said.

The researchers set up a theoretical model looking at how the remote area of the solar system would have evolved over the past four billion years.

"In coming up with an explanation for the celestial bodies, we thought it would be most natural to assume the existence of a yet unknown planet," Mukai said.

"Based on our hypothesis, we calculated how debris moved over the past four billion years. The result matched the actual movement of the celestial bodies we can observe now," he said.

He was hopeful about research by Kobe University, the University of Hawaii and Taiwan's National Central University.

"We are expecting that the ongoing joint celestial observation project will eventually discover Planet X," Mukai said.

The New York Times reported on June 19, 1982 that something out there beyond the farthest reaches of the known solar system seems to be tugging at Uranus and Neptune. Some gravitational force keeps perturbing the two giant planets, causing irregularities in their orbits. The force suggests a presence far away and unseen, a large object that may be the long-sought Planet X.

The last time a serious search of the skies was made it led to the discovery in 1930 of Pluto, the ninth planet. But the story begins more than a century before that, after the discovery of Uranus in 1781 by the English astronomer and musician William Herschel. Until then, the planetary system seemed to end with Saturn.

The discovery of new planets has, in the last two hundred years, owed more to the science of mathematics than it has to the design of bigger and better telescopes. The unaccounted for mathematical irregularities in the orbits of the outer planets have prompted astronomers to speculate upon the existence of a further, undiscovered planet. Astronomers are so certain of this planet's existence that they have already named it Planet X - the Tenth Planet.

NASA themselves officially recognized the possibility of Planet X, with an announcement that "some kind of mystery object is really there – far beyond the outermost planets." One year later, the newly launched IRAS (Infrared Astronomical Satellite) spotted a large mysterious object in the depths of space.

To this day, the search continues for a Planet X...although some say that Planet X has already been found, a planet that matches the Sumerian descriptions for a celestial body 4-8 times the size of earth, on a highly 3,600 elliptical orbit around our sun. In the early 1990's, calculations by the United States Naval Observatory have confirmed the orbital perturbation exhibited by Uranus and Neptune, which Dr. Thomas C Van Flandern, an astronomer at the observatory, says could be explained by "a single undiscovered planet." He and a colleague, Dr. Robert Harrington, calculate that the 10th planet should be two to five times more massive than Earth and have a highly elliptical orbit that takes it some 5 billion miles beyond that of Pluto.

We now know that beyond the giant planets Jupiter and Saturn there are two major planets, Uranus and Neptune, and small proto-planets such as Pluto and Eris. But such knowledge is quite recent.

With the use of improved telescopes, Uranus was discovered in 1781. In 1846, astronomers guided by mathematical calculations pinpointed Neptune. It became evident that Neptune was being subjected to an unknown gravitational pull, and in 1930 Pluto (was located). The latest advances in space imaging do not rely solely on orbital perturbations as the way for locating and identifying possible candidates for Planet X.

The 6,000 year old Sumerian descriptions of our solar system include one more planet they called "Nibiru," which means "Planet of the crossing." The descriptions of this planet by the Sumerians match precisely the specifications of Planet X (the Tenth Planet), which is currently being sought by astronomers in the depths of our own Solar System.

Why has Planet X not been seen in recent times? Views from modern and ancient astronomy, which both suggest a highly elliptical, comet-like orbit, takes Planet X into the depths of space, well beyond the orbit of Pluto. However, there are suggestions that Planet X's orbit could be so eccentric, compared to the rest of the solar system, that its approach would go unnoticed until it was significantly close to the sun. Depending where the Earth was in its orbit, the unexpected close approach of a new planet could have dire consequences.

THE END OF THE WORLD AS WE KNOW IT

Every generation thinks that they just may be the last generation to walk the planet. People seem to have an almost perverse pleasure in frightening themselves into believing that the "end of days" is close at hand. Many hope for the end of the world because it fulfills a desire to see divine punishment for those who are considered sinners, unbelievers, or unworthy. Others hope for the return of deities and the resurrection of long passed loved ones. And there are those who simply cannot conceive the world continuing to exist past their own short life span.

Despite the predictions, despite the prophecies, despite the worry, the world continues to spin in its orbit and life goes on. But people cannot help but to look apprehensively towards the future. Surely something will happen someday...someone pushes the wrong button, sending nuclear-tipped missiles flying...a plague will strike...a comet will hit...a nearby star will go supernova. There are just so many things that can go wrong that statistically, the chances are pretty good that something bad <u>will</u> occur someday.

When the end of the world does come about, and everything is left a smoking ruin; it is almost a certainty that there will be someone left to shout to the smoldering ashes, "I Told You So!" Religioustolerance.org has compiled an excellent list of people who once were certain that they knew exactly when the apocalypse would come.

<u>About 30 CE:</u> The Christian Scriptures (New Testament), when interpreted literally, appear to record many predictions by Jeshua of Nazareth (Jesus Christ) that God's Kingdom would arrive within a very short period, or was actually in the process of arriving. For example, Jesus is recorded as saying in Matthew 16:28: "...there shall be some standing here, which shall not taste of death, till they see the Son of Man coming in his kingdom." In Matthew 24:34, Yeshua is recorded as saying: "...This generation shall not pass, till all these things be fulfilled." Since the life expectancy in those days was little over 30 years, Jesus appears to have predicted his second coming sometime during the 1st century CE. It didn't happen.

About 60 CE: Interpreting the Epistles of Paul of Tarsus literally, his writings seem to imply that Jesus would return and usher in rapture during the lifetime of persons who were living in the middle of the 1st century.

<u>About 90 CE:</u> Saint Clement 1 predicted that the world end would occur at any moment.

<u>2nd Century CE:</u> Prophets and Prophetesses of the Montanist movement predicted that Jesus would return sometime during their lifetime and establish the New Jerusalem in the city of Pepuza in Asia Minor.

<u>365 CE:</u> A man by the name of Hilary of Poitiers, announced that the end would happen that year.

375 to 400 CE: Saint Martin of Tours, a student of Hilary, was convinced that the end would happen sometime before 400 CE.

500 CE: The antipope Hippolytus and an earlier Christian academic Sextus Julius Africanus had predicted Armageddon at about this year.

968 CE: An eclipse was interpreted as a prelude to the end of the world by the army of the German emperor Otto III.

992 CE: Good Friday coincided with the Feast of the Annunciation; this had long been believed to be the event that would bring forth the Antichrist, and thus the end-times events foretold in the book of Revelation. Records from Germany report that a new sun rose in the north and that as many as three suns and three moons were fighting.

1000, Jan. 1: Many Christians in Europe had predicted the return of Jesus and his kingdom. As the date approached, Christian armies waged war against some of the Pagan countries in Northern Europe. The motivation was to convert them all to Christianity, by force if necessary, before Christ returned in the year 1000. Meanwhile, some Christians had given their possessions to the Church in anticipation of the end. Fortunately, the level of education was so low that many citizens were unaware of the year. They did not know enough to be afraid. Otherwise, the panic might have been far worse than it was.

1000, May: The body of Charlemagne was disinterred on Pentecost. A legend had arisen that an emperor would rise from his sleep to fight the Antichrist.

1005-1006: A terrible famine throughout Europe was seen as a sign of the nearness of the end.

1033: Some believed this to be the 1000th anniversary of the death and resurrection of Jesus. His second coming was anticipated. Jesus' actual date of execution is unknown, but is believed to be in the range of 27 to 33 CE.

Out Of The Darkness – UFO Revelations And Planet X

THE FOUR HORSEMEN OF THE APOCALYPSE

1147: Gerard of Poehlde decided that the millennium had actually started in 306 CE during Constantine's reign. Thus, the world end was expected in 1306 CE.

1179: John of Toledo predicted the end of the world during 1186. This estimate was based on the alignment of many planets.

1205: Joachim of Fiore predicted in 1190 that the Antichrist was already in the world, and that King Richard of England would defeat him. The Millennium would then begin, sometime before 1205.

1284: Pope Innocent III computed this date by adding 666 years onto the date the Islam was founded.

1346 and later: The black plague spread across Europe, killing one third of the population. This was seen as the prelude to an immediate end of the world.

1496: This was approximately 1500 years after the birth of Jesus. Some mystics in the 15th century predicted that the millennium would begin during this year.

1524: Many astrologers predicted the imminent end of the world due to a world wide flood.

1533: Melchior Hoffman predicted that Jesus' return would happen a millennium and a half after the nominal date of his execution, in 1533. The New Jerusalem was expected to be established in Strasbourg, Germany. He was arrested and died in a Strasbourg jail.

1669: The Old Believers in Russia believed that the end of the world would occur in this year. 20 thousand burned themselves to death between 1669 and 1690 to protect themselves from the Antichrist.

1689: Benjamin Keach, a 17th century Baptist, predicted the end of the world for this year.

1736: British theologian and mathematician William Whitson predicted a great flood similar to Noah's for October 13 of this year.

Out Of The Darkness – UFO Revelations And Planet X

<u>1792</u>: This was the date of the end of the world calculated by some believers in the Shaker movement.

<u>1794</u>: Charles Wesley, one of the founders of Methodism, thought Doomsday would be in this year.

<u>1830</u>: Margaret McDonald, a Christian prophetess, predicted that Robert Owen would be the Antichrist. Owen helped found New Harmony, Indiana.

<u>1843, March, 21</u>: William Miller, founder of the Millerite movement, predicted that Jesus would come on this date. A very large number of Christians accepted his prophecy.

<u>1844, Oct. 22</u>: When Jesus did not return, Miller predicted this new date. In an event which is now called "he Great Disappointment," many Christians sold their property and possessions, quit their jobs and prepared themselves for the second coming. Nothing happened; the day came and went without incident.

<u>1850</u>: Ellen White, founder of the Seven Day Adventists movement, made many predictions of the timing of the end of the world.

<u>1891</u>: Mother Shipton, a 16th century mystic predicted the end of the world: "...The world to an end shall come; in eighteen hundred and eighty-one."

<u>1891 or before</u>: On Feb. 14, 1835, Joseph Smith, the founder of the Mormon church, attended a meeting of church leaders. He said that the meeting had been called because God had commanded it. He announced that Jesus would return within 56 years – i.e. before 1891. (History of the Church 2:182)

<u>1914</u> was one of the more important estimates of the start of the war of Armageddon by the Jehovah's Witnesses (Watchtower Bible and Tract Society). They based their prophecy of 1914 from prophecy in the book of Daniel, Chapter 4. The writings referred to "seven times." The WTS interpreted each "time" as equal to 360 days, giving a total of 2520 days. This was further interpreted as representing 2520 years, measured from the starting date of 607 BCE. This gave 1914 as the target date. When 1914 passed, they changed their prediction; 1914 became the year that Jesus invisibly began his rule.

Out Of The Darkness – UFO Revelations And Planet X

1914, 1915, 1918, 1920, 1925, 1941, 1975 and 1994, etc. were other dates that the Watchtower Society (WTS) or its members predicted. Since late in the 19th century, they had taught that the "battle of the Great Day of God Almighty" (Armageddon) would happen in 1914 CE.

The next major estimate was 1925. Watchtower magazine predicted: "The year 1925 is a date definitely and clearly marked in the Scriptures, even more clearly than that of 1914; but it would be presumptuous on the part of any faithful follower of the Lord to assume just what the Lord is going to do during that year."

The Watchtower Society selected 1975 as its next main prediction. This was based on the estimate "according to reliable Bible chronology Adam was created in the year 4026 BCE, likely in the autumn of the year, at the end of the sixth day of creation." They believed that the year 1975 a promising date for the end of the world, as it was the 6,000th anniversary of Adam's creation. Exactly 1,000 years was to pass for each day of the creation week. This prophecy also failed.

The current estimate is that the end of the world as we know it will happen precisely 6000 years after the creation of Eve.

<u>1919</u>: Meteorologist Albert Porta predicted that the conjunction of 6 planets would generate a magnetic current that would cause the sun to explode and engulf the Earth on Dec. 17.

<u>1936</u>: Herbert W Armstrong, founder of the Worldwide Church of God, predicted that the Day of the Lord would happen sometime in 1936. When the prediction failed, he made a new estimate: 1975.

<u>1940 or 1941</u>: A Bible teacher from Australia, Leonard Sale-Harrison, held a series of prophesies conferences across North America in the 1930's. He predicted that the end of the world would happen in 1940 or 1941.

<u>1948</u>: During this year, the state of Israel was founded. Some Christians believed that this event was the final prerequisite for the second coming of Jesus. Various end of the world predictions were made in the range 1888 to 2048.

<u>1953</u>: David Davidson wrote a book titled *The Great Pyramid, Its Divine Message*. In it, he predicted that the world would end in August.

<u>1957</u>: The Watchtower magazine quoted a pastor from California, Mihran Ask, as saying: "Sometime between April 16 and

23, 1957, Armageddon will sweep the world! Millions of persons will perish in its flames and the land will be scorched."

1959: Florence Houteff's, who was the leader of the Branch Davidians faith group, prophesied that the 1260 days mentioned in Revelation 11:3 would end and the Kingdom of David would be established in 1959. Followers expected to die, be resurrected, and transferred to Heaven. Many sold their possessions and moved to Mt. Carmel in anticipation of the "end time." When nothing happened, most of the congregation left. Only a few dozen members remained.

1960: Piazzi Smyth, a past astronomer royal of Scotland, wrote a book circa 1860 titled *Our Inheritance in the Great Pyramid*. He concluded from his research that the millennium would start before the end of 1960 CE.

1967: During the six day war, the Israeli army captured all of Jerusalem. Many conservative Christians believed that the rapture would occur quickly. However, the final Biblical prerequisite for the second coming is that the Jews resume ritual animal sacrifices in the temple at Jerusalem. So far, that has not happened.

1970's: The late Moses David (formerly David Berg) was the founder of the Christian religious group, The Children of God. He predicted that a comet would hit the earth, probably in the mid 1970's and destroy all life in the United States. One source indicated that he believed it would happen in 1973.

1972: According to an article in the *Atlantic Magazine*, "Herbert W. Armstrong's empire suffered a serious blow when the end failed to begin in January of 1972, as Armstrong had predicted, thus bringing hardship to many people who had given most of their assets to the church in the expectation of going to Petra, where such worldly possessions would be useless.
"The failure of this prophetic scenario to take place according to this Co-Worker letter scenario, which was often repeated over the years in print by Armstrong, may have been one of the initial reasons why the church organization began to decline as unfulfilled expectations led to great disappointment. As events unfolded, it became obvious 1972 did not have the biblical significance that the church had anticipated for nearly two decades."

1974: Charles Meade, a pastor in Daleville, Indiana, predicted that the end of the world will happen during his lifetime. He was born circa 1927, so the end will probably come early in the 21st century.

1975: Many Jehovah's Witness predicted this date. However, it was not officially recognized by the leadership.

1978: Chuck Smith, Pastor of Calvary Chapel in Cost Mesa, CA, predicted the rapture in 1981.

1980: Leland Jensen leader of a Baha'i Faith group predicted that a nuclear disaster would happen in 1980. This would be followed by two decades of conflict, ending in the establishment of God's Kingdom on Earth.

1981: Rev. Sun Myung Moon, founder of the Unification Church predicted that the Kingdom of Heaven would be established this year.

1982: Pat Robertson predicted a few years in advance that the world would end in the fall of 1982.

1982: Astronomers John Gribben & Setphen Plagemann predicted the *Jupiter Effect* in 1974. They wrote that when various planets were aligned on the same side of the sun, tidal forces would create solar flares, radio interruptions, rainfall and temperature disturbances and massive earthquakes. The planets did align as seen from earth, as they do regularly.

1984 to 1999: In 1983, Bhagwan Shree Rajneesh, later called Osho, teacher of what has been called the Rajneesh movement, is said to have predicted massive destruction on earth, including natural disasters and man-made catastrophes. Floods larger than any since Noah, extreme earthquakes, very destructive volcano eruptions, nuclear wars etc. were to happen. Tokyo, New York, San Francisco, Los Angeles, Bombay will all disappear.

1985: Arnold Murray of the Shepherd's Chapel predicted that the war of Armageddon will start on June 8-9 in "a valley of the Alaskan peninsula."

1986: Moses David of The Children of God faith group predicted that the Battle of Armageddon would take place in 1986. Russia would defeat Israel and the United States. A worldwide Communist dictatorship would be established. In 1993, Christ would return to earth.

Out Of The Darkness – UFO Revelations And Planet X

<u>1987 to 2000</u>: Lester Sumrall, in his 1987 book, *I Predict 2000 AD*, predicted that Jerusalem would be the richest city on Earth, that the Common Market would rule Europe, and that there would be a nuclear war involving Russia and perhaps the U.S. Also, he prophesized that the greatest Christian revival in the history of the church would happen: all during the last 13 years of the 20th century.

<u>1988</u>: Hal Lindsey had predicted in his book *The Late, Great Planet Earth* that the Rapture was coming in 1988 – one generation or 40 years after the creation of the state of Israel.

<u>1988</u>: Edgar Whisenaut, a NASA scientist, had published the book *88 Reasons why the Rapture will Occur in 1988*. It sold over four million copies.

<u>About 1990</u>: Peter Ruckman concluded from his analysis of the Bible that the rapture would come within a few years of 1990.

<u>1991</u>: Nation of Islam Leader Louis Farrakhan proclaimed the Gulf War would to be "the War of Armageddon...the final War."

<u>1992</u>: A Korean group called Mission for the Coming Days had the Korea Church a buzz in the fall of 1992. They foresaw Oct 28, 1992 as the time for the Rapture. Numerology was the basis for the date. Several camera shots that left ghostly images on pictures were thought to be a supernatural confirmation of the date.

<u>Oct. 28, 1992</u>: Full page ad in USA Today, on Oct. 20, 1991, placed by the Hyoo-go (Rapture) movement. Supposedly, 50 million people will die in earthquakes, 50 million from collapsed buildings, 1.4 billion from World War III and 1.4 billion from a separate Armageddon.

<u>1993</u>: If the year 2000 is the end of the 6000 year cycle, then the rapture must take place in 1993, because you would need seven years of the tribulation. This was the thinking of a number of prophecy writers.

<u>1994</u>: Even though they announced that they would not make any more end time predictions, the Jehovah's Witnesses proclaimed 1994 as the conclusion of an 80 year generation - the year 1914 was the starting point.

Out Of The Darkness – UFO Revelations And Planet X

Oct. 23, 1996: Since 1658, many Christians have accepted the calculations of James Ussher, an Irish archbishop, who estimated that the first day of creation occurred on 4004-OCT-23 BCE. This would make the time interval between the creation of the world and a common estimate of the birth of Christ to be precisely 4000 years. Some people believe that Ussher fudged the data to make it come out neatly. He also estimated that the end of the world would occur exactly 6000 years later, in the fall of 1996.

1997-1999: Russian scientist Vladimir Sobolyovhas of the Rerikh Academy has analyzed prophesies made by Russian saints, by Nostradamus etc. He announced his conclusions in 1997: that the Earth's axis will suddenly tilt about 30 degrees sometime during the next two years. This will submerge the Scandinavian countries and Britain under water, in what is termed the Armageddon Flood. Siberia will be spared. He expects that aliens will intervene and lead the world into the fourth dimension. Right now, these aliens are on Earth, but in hiding. Sobolyovhas said: "If we completely believed in them, we would get lazy. So they are clever. They stay hidden in the fourth dimension and only show themselves from time to time."

1998: A Taiwanese cult operating out of Garland, Texas predicted Christ would return on Mar 31, 1998. The group's leader, Heng-ming Chen, announced God would return, and then invite the cult members aboard a UFO. The group abandoned their second coming prediction when a precursor event failed to take place. The cult's leader said God would appear on every channel 18 of every TV in the world, but it never happend.

1999: A group known as "Concerned Christians," whose members were ordered deported from Israel, was started by Monte Kim Miller, who used to run an anti-cult network in Denver. Miller believed he was the last prophet on Earth before Armageddon. Miller also claimed that America was Satan and the government evil. Miller predicted he would die on the streets of Jerusalem in December 1999 and would rise from the dead three days later.

2000: Michael Drosnin, author of *The Bible Code*, found a hidden message in the Pentateuch (the first five books in the Bible) that predicts that World War III, involving a worldwide nuclear holocaust, will start in 2000.

Jan. 1, 2000: William Cooper, head of a militia group in St. John's AZ, predicted that on this date the secret chambers of the

Out Of The Darkness – UFO Revelations And Planet X

Pyramid at Giza will be opened. Its secrets will be revealed and Satan will become a public figure. The American militia will engage in a massive war at this time.

<u>2001</u>: Charles Spiegel, a retired psychology professor, preaches from a small town near San Diego, California that the ancient land of Atlantis will emerge from the Caribbean circa 2001 CE. Shortly thereafter, 1000 extraterrestrials from "Myton" in 33 spaceships will land there and bring new knowledge to humanity.

<u>2004</u>: Arnie Stanton noted that on Sep. 16, 1997 it was the fourth Jewish festival since Apr. 3, 1996 on which a lunar eclipse occurred. He quoted Luke 21:25-26 which mentions "signs in the sun, in the moon and in the stars and on the earth distress of nations" He believed that "these recent lunar eclipses are the last known astronomical signs that will precede a seven year (360 day/year) countdown to Armageddon/Christ's return to the Earth." He expects that Christ's return will occur within a few months of Sep. 2004 when Asteroid Toutatis comes dangerously close to the Earth.

<u>2008</u>: Ronald Weinland in his book *God's Final Witness*, writes that: "A little after April, a dollar bill won't be worth anything...we're going to be brought down the tubes, very quickly...What happens when a nuclear weapon goes off in New York and Chicago? By the fall of 2011, that's when Jesus Christ returns."

<u>2012</u>: Mayan and Aztec calendars predicted the end of the age on Dec 21, 2012. Also, Michael Drosnin, author of *The Bible Code*, found a hidden message in the Pentateuch (the first five books in the Bible) that predicts that a comet will crash into the Earth in 2012 and annihilate all life. Of course this did not happen.

So how do true believers react when it's clear that the world didn't end? More often the failed prophecy actually makes their belief stronger. Believers may rationalize away the failure in one or more of the following ways: They may decide that the end is in fact near, but that the time or date was simply misinterpreted and move the true end-times date forward. They may decide that their faith and prayer actually saved the world and averted disaster; or they may believe that the end of the world did in fact occur, but nobody else noticed it because it was a spiritual apocalypse, not a physical one.

Which brings us back to Planet X...Is Planet X making a beeline for the inner solar system bringing with it death, destruction and chaos? Is the end of the world finally going to happen? A lot of people think so and have offered all kinds of interesting evidence to back up their claims.

At any rate, history has shown us that despite the dire warnings, the world is still here. However, simply because the world has not ended yet is no excuse for becoming complacent and foolhardy. Bad things do happen – usually when we least expect it.

Even though we have tried to remain diligent and alert in the face of potential disaster; there is no doubt that someday we will be caught completely by surprise when the time we have all dreaded looms before us and catastrophe is certain.

Art By Carol Rodriguez

CHAPTER TWO
What Is Planet X?

Planet X is thought to be the tenth planet in the solar system. The average solar system is binary (has two suns) and has a dwarf that orbits back and forth or around the two suns. Our solar system is average in both regards. It is believed that the space probes Pioneers 10 and 11 found Planet X along with the dark star twin sun and considerable effort has been made to keep this information from the public. Its orbit around the two suns takes approximately 3600-3700 years to complete one cycle.

When Planet X enters our immediate solar system, its effects are far reaching, even at a distance. As it draws closer, the sun regularly erupts with major solar flares, even during a solar minimum. Considerable solar energy reaches Earth and interplay begins between the electromagnetic fields of the planets.

Some of the earliest effects are unusual changes in the weather, an increase in seismic and volcanic activity, and melting of the polar icecaps. These symptoms are being blamed on manmade conditions that produce global warming. However, there is evidence that global warming is also occurring on Mars and other planets in the solar system.

The closer Planet X gets to Earth, the more dramatic are its effects. It is believed that ice ages, were in fact pole shifts, the gravitational pull upon our core, during a close approach of Planet X can be great enough to dislodge the crust, resulting in a pole shift.

Perhaps we have already been warned that something disastrous is about to happen. Robert Boerman, a Dutch Crop Circle researcher, wrote in his book *Crop Circles, Gods and Their Secrets*, that an analysis of crop formations reveals a Kabalistic code that provides clues about Nibiru, or Planet X. This planet is in a huge elliptical orbit, which, according to Zecharia Sitchin's translations of cuneiform tablets from Sumeria, returns to our solar system every 3,600 years, and houses the "gods" who cross-bred our ancestors by genetic engineering.

Out Of The Darkness – UFO Revelations And Planet X

Boerman was constantly finding precessional numbers in his analysis of crop formations, and goes on to calculate, following some of the leads given by Alan Alford in *Gods of the New Millennium*, that Nibiru is due to return to the solar system in 2012, when the Mayan Great cycle ends.

One would imagine that if a large planet or some other celestial body were heading towards us, we would have seen it by now. But NASA seems to be silent about Planet X, and they certainly are not warning anyone to prepare for its passage. So that must mean that we have nothing to worry about...or do we?

Actually, NASA was the first to announce the discovery of Planet X, back in 1980s as reported in the June 19, 1982 edition of the New York Times:

> Something out there beyond the furthest reaches of the known solar system is tugging at Uranus and Neptune. A gravitational force keeps perturbing the two giant planets, causing irregularities in their orbits. The force suggests a presence far away and unseen, a large object, the long-sought Planet X. Astronomers are so certain of this planet's existence that they have already named it 'Planet X - the 10th Planet.'

However, someone must have decided that this was information that was best kept secret because within a week NASA retracted their announcement and have been publicly silent ever since. Nevertheless, there is strong evidence that they have had an internal project tracking Planet X as this NASA internal document records:

> NASA ADS Astronomy Abstract Service
> Find Similar Abstracts (with default settings below)
> Also-Read Articles · Translate Abstract
> Title: *Search for planet X*
> Authors: Harrington, Robert S.
> Affiliation: Naval Observatory, Washington, DC.
> Journal: In NASA, Washington, Reports of Planetary Astronomy, 1991 p. 53 (SEE N92-12792 03-89)
> Publication Date: 10/1991
> Category: Astronomy
> Origin: STI
> NASA/STI Keywords: PERTURBATION, SKY SURVEYS (ASTRONOMY), SOLAR ORBITS, SPACE OBSERVATIONS (FROM EARTH), NEPTUNE (PLANET), URANUS (PLANET)
> Bibliographic Code: 1991plas.rept...53H

Out Of The Darkness – UFO Revelations And Planet X

Abstract:
The observation of the region of the sky in which it is believed Planet X should now be, based on perturbations observed in the motions of Uranus and Neptune, was determined, and there was no reason to update that determination. A limited area of that region was photographed, and that will be continued. A given area is photographed with the twin 20 cm astrograph in New Zealand on two successive nights near the time that area is in opposition, and these plates are blinked in Washington to identify anything that has moved. The predicted region is in the south, which requires observations from a southern station, and it is in opposition in the April to June period, which means observations have not yet started for the year. Blinking will be done as soon as the plates are received in Washington.

http://adsabs.harvard.edu

Author James McCanney has dealt closely with NASA during his career and says that the agency is under congressional order not to tell the public if they discover a doomsday scenario. This is the same edict that restrains public officials from telling the public of an impending disaster and causing a panic.

If we accept that NASA knows about Planet X but is keeping the public in the dark about it because of national security issues, what about the amateur astronomers and institutions of other countries who are not restricted in that way? Why are they not reporting Planet X?

Once again, according to McCanney, Planet X's lack of brightness and position make it difficult to see. Its current location makes it visible only in the spring, and because of its skewed elliptical orbit, Planet X is approaches our solar system from below the ecliptic (plane of the planets' orbits) meaning the best viewing is in Antarctica.

Even someone from NASA has admitted that there is a very strong probability of being caught by surprise by something unexpectedly flying in from outer space. David Morrison, Director of Space & Astrobiology at NASA's Ames Research Center has spoken before Congress on the threat of cosmic impacts. He writes: "It is possible for a comet to 'sneak up' on Earth, escaping detection until it is only a few weeks from impact. A perpetual survey is required to detect long-period comets, and even with such a survey we cannot be sure of success."

Out Of The Darkness – UFO Revelations And Planet X

The odds of Planet X directly hitting us are remote. Unfortunately, an impact is not necessary to cause major problems. Because of the gravity and magnetism of Planet X it will be able to disrupt things on our planet from a distance, just as it is allegedly already been doing to the solar system.

Planet X could cause the Earth to flip its poles...north would become south and vice versa. This is caused by a gravitational tidal wave that moves through the surface mantle of the Earth. There would be horrible earthquakes, volcanoes, and flooding caused by tidal waves and storms.

If you have any doubts that this scenario is even possible, take a close look at the orbits of some of the other planets in the solar system. David J. Tholen of the University of Hawaii says that Pluto was probably hit by another in the not-too-distant past. One consequence of that collision, he argues, is seen in the planet's motion — Pluto and its satellite Charon now waltz around each other in slightly out-of-round orbits. And since tidal forces in the tight planet-moon system should damp out any deviations from purely circular orbits within 10 million years or so, the impact must have occurred relatively recently.

Tholen says that a mere close encounter, and not a direct impact, with another celestial body would do the trick. But a direct hit is not so far-fetched.

"Impacts do happen," Tholen stresses, noting Comet Shoemaker-Levy 9's fateful encounter with Jupiter in 1994.

CHAPTER THREE
Planet X And The Mayan Calendar

So what is the Mayan Calendar? The calendar was constructed by an advanced civilization called the Mayans around 250-900 C.E. Evidence for the Maya empire stretches around most parts of the southern states of Mexico and reaches down to the current geological locations of Guatemala, Belize, El Salvador and some of Honduras. The people living in Mayan society exhibited very advanced written skills and had an amazing ability when constructing cities and urban planning. The Mayans are probably most famous for their pyramids and other intricate and grand buildings. The people of Maya had a huge impact on Central American culture, not just within their civilization, but with other indigenous populations in the region. Significant numbers of Mayans still live today, continuing their age-old traditions.

The Mayans used many different calendars and viewed time as a meshing of spiritual cycles. While the calendars had practical uses, such as social, agricultural, commercial and administrative tasks, there was a very heavy religious element. Each day had a patron spirit, signifying that each day had specific use. This contrasts greatly with our modern Gregorian calendar which primarily sets the administrative, social and economic dates.

Most of the Mayan calendars were short. The Tzolk'in calendar lasted for 260 days and the Haab' approximated the solar year of 365 days. The Mayans then combined both the Tzolk'in and the Haab' to form the "Calendar Round," a cycle lasting 52 Haab's (around 52 years, or the approximate length of a generation). Within the Calendar Round were the trecena (13 day cycle) and the veintena (20 day cycle). Obviously, this system would only be of use when considering the 18,980 unique days over the course of 52 years. In addition to these systems, the Mayans also had the "Venus Cycle." Being keen and highly accurate astronomers they formed a calendar based on the location of Venus in the night sky. It's also possible they did the same with the other planets in the Solar System.

Using the Calendar Round is an excellent way to remember the date of a birthday or significant religious periods, but what about recording history? There was no way to record a date older than 52 years.

The Mayans had a solution. Using an innovative method, they were able to expand on the 52 year Calendar Round. Up to this point, the Mayan Calendar may have sounded a little archaic – after all, it was possibly based on religious belief, mathematical calculations using the numbers 13 and 20 as the base units and a heavy mix of astrological myth. The only principal correlation with the modern calendar is the Haab' that recognized there were 365 days in one solar year (it's not clear whether the Mayans accounted for leap years). The answer to a longer calendar could be found in the "Long Count," a calendar lasting 5126 years.

The base year for the Mayan Long Count starts at "0.0.0.0.0." Each zero goes from 0-19 and each represent a tally of Mayan days. So, for example, the first day in the Long Count is denoted as 0.0.0.0.1. On the 19th day we'll have 0.0.0.0.19, on the 20th day it goes up one level and we'll have 0.0.0.1.0. This count continues until 0.0.1.0.0 (about one year), 0.1.0.0.0 (about 20 years) and 1.0.0.0.0 (about 400 years). Therefore, if an arbitrary date of 2.10.12.7.1 is picked, this represents the Mayan date of approximately 1012 years, 7 months and 1 day.

The Mayan Prophecy is wholly based on the assumption that something bad is going to happen when the Mayan Long Count calendar runs out. Experts are divided as to when the Long Count ends, but as the Maya used the numbers of 13 and 20 at the root of their numerical systems, the last day could occur on 13.0.0.0.0. This date represents 5126 years and the Long Count started on 0.0.0.0.0, which corresponds to the modern date of August 11th 3114 BC. The Mayan Long Count therefore ends 5126 years later on December 21, 2012.

When something ends (even something as innocent as an ancient calendar), people seem to think up the most extreme possibilities for the end of civilization as we know it. Archaeologists and mythologists believe that the Mayans predicted an age of enlightenment, a religious miracle, when 13.0.0.0.0 comes around.

The Mayans prophesied that starting from 1999 we have 13 years to realize the changes in our conscious attitude and to stop our self-destructive ways. We then need to move onto a path that opens our consciousness to integrate with the universe. The Mayans knew that our Sun, or Kinich-Ahau, every so often synchronized with the central of our galaxy, the Milky Way. From this center will come a "spark" of light/energy which causes the Sun to shine more intensely producing solar flares and changes in the Sun's magnetic field. The Mayans say that this happens every 5,125 years, but also that this causes a displacement in the Earth's rotation, which also creates great catastrophes from Earth changes such as shifts in the Poles.

The Mayans believed the universal processes, like the "breathing" of the galaxy, are cycles that never change. What changes is the consciousness of man that passes through it, always in a process toward more perfection. Based on their observations, the Mayans predicted that from the initial date of the start of their civilization, 4 Ahau, 8 Cumku which is 3113 B.C., after one cycle being completed 5,125 years in their future, December 21, 2012.

The Sun, having received a powerful ray of synchronizing light from the center of the galaxy, would change its polarity which would produce a great cosmic event that would propel human kind to be ready to cross into a new era, The Golden Age. It is after this, that the Mayans say we will be ready to go through the door that was left by them, transforming our current civilization, which is based on fear, to a higher harmonic vibration.

Only from our individual efforts can we avoid the path to great cataclysms that our planet will suffer at the start of the new era. In the last cataclysm of the Mayas, their civilization was destroyed by a great flood that left few survivors. Our Biblical story of Noah's great flood is our ancestral memory from this time. The Maya believed that having known the end of their cycle, mankind can prepare for what is to come. The Maya believed that the coming changes will permit us to make a quantum leap forward in the evolution of our consciousness to create a new civilization that will manifest great harmony and compassion to all humankind.

Their first prophecy talks about "The Time of No-Time," a period of 20 years, which they call a Katún. The last 20 years of the Sun's cycle of 5,125 years, this cycle is from 1992 - 2012. They predicted that during these times, solar winds would become more intense, and that this would be a time of great realization and great change for mankind. It would also be a time when mankind realizes the damage it has done to the planet through pollution, greed and a lack of respect for the beauty of our world. According to the Mayans, these changes will happen so that mankind comprehends how the universe works and allow us to advance to superior levels, leaving behind superficial materialism and liberating ourselves from suffering.

The Mayans say, that seven years after the start of Katún, 1999, we would enter a time of darkness which would force us to confront our own conduct. They say that this is the time when mankind will enter "The Sacred Hall of Mirrors," where we will look at ourselves and analyze our behaviors with ourselves, with others, with nature and with the planet in which we live.

This is a time in which all of humanity, by individual conscious decision, decides to change and eliminate fear and lack of respect from all of our relationships. The Mayans prophesied that the start of this period would be marked by a solar eclipse on August 11, 1999, known to them as 13 Ahau, 8 Cauac, and would coincide with an unprecedented planetary alignment, the "Grand Cross" alignment.

This would be the last 13 years of the Katón period; the last opportunity for our civilization to realize the changes that are coming at the moment of our spiritual regeneration. For the Mayans, everything is numbers and the time of the 13 sacred numbers started in August 1999. They predicted that along with the eclipse, the forces of nature would act like a catalyst of changes so accelerated and with such magnitude that mankind would be powerless against them. Also, that our technologies in which we rely on so much would begin to fail us.

We will no longer be able to learn from our civilization in the way that we are organized as a society. They said that our internal, spiritual development would require a better place along with a better way to interact with more respect and compassion. The first prophecies were attained by the Maya's study of the Sun. They discovered that the entire solar system moved that even our universe has its own cycles, repetitive periods which begin and end like our day and night.

These discoveries lead to the understanding that our solar system rotates on an ellipse that brings our solar system closer and further from the center of the galaxy. In other words, according to the Mayans, our Sun and all of its planets rotate in cycles in relation to the center of the galaxy or Hunab-Kú, the central light of the galaxy.

It takes 25,625 years for our solar system to make one cycle on this ellipse. One complete cycle is called a galactic day. The cycle is divided into two halves similar to our day and night. The half closest to the central light, is our solar system's 'day' and the half furthest away is its "night." Each day and each night lasts 12,800 years, meaning that the central galaxy is the Sun for our entire solar system.

The Mayans discovered that every grand cycle has its minor cycles that carry the same characteristics. One galactic day of 25,625 years is divided into five cycles of 5,125 years. The first cycle is the galactic morning, when our solar system is just coming out of the darkness to enter the light.

The second cycle is the midday, when our solar system is closest to the central light. The third cycle is the afternoon, when our solar system begins to come out of the light. The fourth cycle is the late-night, when our solar system has entered its furthest cycle from the central light. And the fifth and last cycle is night before dawn, when our solar system is in its last cycle of darkness before starting again. This is the cycle we are currently coming out of.

The Mayan prophecy tells us that in 1999, our solar system began to leave the end of the fifth cycle which started in 3113 B.C. and that we find ourselves in the morning of our galactic day, exiting darkness and on the verge of being in plain day of our central galaxy in 2012. They say that at the beginning and end of these cycles, which is to say, every 5,125 years, the central sun or light of the galaxy emits a ray of light so intense and so brilliant that it illuminates the entire universe. It is from this burst of light that all of the Suns and planets sync.

The Mayans compare this burst to the life pulse of the universe, beating once every 5,125 years, each life pulse lasting 20 years, a Katún. These pulses mark the end of one cycle and the beginning of the next. So we come back to what they call "The Time of No Time," an evolutionary period, short but intense, inside the grand cycles where great changes take place to thrust us into a new age of evolution as individuals and as mankind. The Mayans believed that after 2012, we as individuals, we will have to make decisions that will affect all of humanity.

WHO WERE THE MAYA?

The story of the Maya begins during the Fourth Ice Age about 60,000 years ago. At this time the earth's ice caps were much larger than today, glaciers extended as far south as the central United States and no tropical climate existed anywhere on our planet. The so-called tropics were covered with savannah and grassland. So much water was trapped in the ice caps that the level of the sea was lower than today and a land bridge about 1,000 miles wide connecting Asia and North America at the Bering Strait was exposed.

The first humans to inhabit the Americas came across this land bridge. At first, travel south was impeded by vast walls of ice but gradually, as the ice melted, people began to spread south.

It is believed the first humans reached Central America about 15,000 years ago. The first identifiable culture, Clovis, existed around 10,000 B.C.E. Some stone tools dating back to 9,000 BC have been found in Guatemala. Around this time, the Fourth Ice Age was drawing to a close and the climate was gradually warming up enabling humans to begin eating more plants and less meat. This change was underway around 8,000 BC.

From 8,000 B.C.E. to 2,000 B.C.E. the inhabitants of Central America gradually became more agrarian and they domesticated beans, corn, peppers, squash and other plants. During this time there was still no jungle, just savannah and grassland and some trees. Evidence indicates that a tropical jungle climate appeared in Central America only quite recently, after the Mayan civilization was well underway. Towards the end of this period, some recognizably Mayan villages appeared and pottery and ceramics appeared. Some villages had a temple. The period from 1500 B.C.E. to 300 C.E. is called the "Pre-Classic" period of Mayan culture. During this period the Mayan language developed. The Mayans experienced population growth and larger towns were constructed.

Meanwhile, the Olmec culture was developing in southern Mexico. The Olmec is viewed as the "mother culture" in Central America; they developed a system of writing, the long-count calendar and a complex religion. The Olmecs had a considerable influence on the fledgling Maya culture. The Maya adopted many of the Olmec skills and practices and developed them further. It seems that the mixture of the Olmec and Mayan cultures touched off an explosion of cultural development. Archaeologists are not sure of the cause but from 300 B.C.E. to 300 C.E., tremendous development occurred in architecture, writing, and calendrics throughout Mayan lands and the population increased. The great cities of El Mirador, Kaminaljuyú, Río Azúl and Tikal all were founded during this time. Mayan cities often went to war against each other.

No sooner had Maya civilization been fairly set upon its feet than it began to progress with extraordinary rapidity. Regarding the precise place of its origin authoritative opinion is practically agreed. The general character of the architectural remains in the region lying between the Bay of Tabasco and the foot of the Cordilleras and watered by the river Usumacinta and the Rio de la Pasion in the modern state of Chiapas, points conclusively to this district as the first settlement of Central American civilization, and the relatively archaic type of the hieroglyphs found upon its monuments as well as the early dates these contain give to this theory something of finality.

The oldest centers of Maya life are probably Tikal and Peten in Eastern Guatemala. It is believed that the development of the southern Maya states continued for nearly four hundred years, or until the close of the sixth century C.E., about which time disaster seems to have come upon them with tragic suddenness. We do not know the cause of the downfall of what must have been a complex and highly-developed civilization.

Possibly a horde of barbarians from the north swept down upon its settled communities. But even today its gorgeous temples and palaces show no signs of deliberate destruction such as would surely have been evident had they fallen into the hands of savage marauders. More probably these cities were emptied of their inhabitants by one of the migratory impulses which reappear so frequently in American native history.

This theory is rendered possible by the fact that the period of their desertion synchronizes with that of the discovery by the Maya of Yucatan, a region whose wealth in stone probably attracted a nation of builders. But Yucatan is, on the whole, an arid country, and it is still more likely that the retreat of the Maya thence was dictated by the imperative reason of self-preservation or by the command of the tribal gods.

The most important of the older city-states were Palenque, Piedras Negras, Ocosingo, Tikal, Yaxchilan, and Quirigua, sites which are scattered over Southern Mexico and Guatemala, while Copan, perhaps the most important of all, is situated in Honduras, the southern limit of Maya culture, so far as is presently known. Of the later sites in Yucatan, Chichen-Itza was by far the most famous, Mayapan, Uxmal, and Labna barely approaching it in celebrity.

With the discovery of Yucatan a new era opened up for Maya art and social activity. At first the struggle for bare existence on the inhospitable and poorly-irrigated plateau was probably intense. But the ingenious immigrants triumphed over conditions of the unhealthiest kind, and by degrees improved their agricultural knowledge and astronomical science, fixing the revolutionary periods of the planets with accuracy and developing the solar calendar. The Maya Renaissance was fully under way by the end of the tenth century and edifices which recall the palmy days of Palenque and Copan were once more rising all over Yucatan.

About the year 1000 C.E. Chichen-Itza, Uxmal, and Mayapan formed a political confederacy and under the pacific conditions which followed the institution of this league art and science blossomed forth anew. Cities multiplied with astonishing rapidity and the art of sculpture, which had now become merely an adjunct to architecture, achieved an elaboration and intricacy of design unsurpassed, perhaps, by any people in any age.

With the disruption of what may be called the Triple Alliance about the year 1200, an event precipitated by the conspiracy of the ruler of Chichen-Itza against his colleague of Mayapan, a series of disastrous wars ensued which lasted until the country was discovered by the Spaniards. These endless internecine struggles led to the employment of mercenaries from the ruder tribes of Mexico, the presence of whom set an indelible stamp upon Maya art and manners, and we find the graceful Maya sculptors forced to carry out the designs, and even accompanying them with the completely different hieroglyphical inscriptions, of a special Mexican military aristocracy.

Had they placed side by side with these the equivalent Maya characters, modern science would have been provided with an American Rosetta stone, as the Mexican glyphs, unlike those of the Maya, can now be deciphered with a reasonable degree of certainty. This brings us to the problem of Maya writing, which is still almost entirely a closed book to investigators. For the pursuit of this quest a far greater degree of industry and ingenuity has been needful than for the decipherment of the ancient writings of Egypt or Sumeria.

Certain of the "calculiform" or pebble-shaped characters have been deciphered, especially those which apply to the sun, moon, and planets, those for "beginning," "ending," the symbols for the year, "night," and the glyphs for the "months" and "days."

The glyphs appear as a number of small squares rounded at the corners and representing human faces and other objects highly conventionalized by generations of artistic usage. They are arranged as a rule in two parallel columns and are read two columns at a time, from left to right and top to bottom.

Formerly it was believed that the work of Landa, Bishop of Yucatan, written in 1565, contained the "key" to the script. But it is now known that the natives, exasperated at his destruction of their manuscripts, deliberately deceived him and that with the exception of the symbols for the days and "months" his "key" is quite misleading.

Much difference of opinion exists as to whether the system is phonetic or ideographic in character. It is probably both phonetic and pictorial to some extent, but for the most part it appears to be of the nature of rebus writing, in which the characters do not indicate the meaning of the objects which they portray, but only the sounds of their names.

Thus, if English were written in this manner, the picture of a human eye might stand for the first personal pronoun, a drawing of a bee for the verb "to be," and so forth. But it seems probable that an ever-increasing number of phonetic elements will be identified, though the idea of a glyph will always be found to overshadow its phonetic value.

Through generations of use the system came to possess a significance entirely ideographic, and would not necessitate any such effort of mental translation as a people unused to rebus writing would have to make in order to comprehend it readily. The manner in which the arithmetical system and dating of the Maya was discovered by Emile Forstemann of Berlin is decidedly the greatest triumph of American archaeology within recent years.

A dot stood for 1 and a bar or line for 5. By various combinations of these the Maya expressed all the numerals from 1 to 19 inclusive. Twenty was denoted by the moon, as indicating the number of days in which the moon waxes and wanes. But the manner in which the higher mathematics of the Maya was evolved is much too intricate a process to be described here.

Each of the periods of time in use among the Maya was based on the period of revolution of one or other of the heavenly bodies and was represented by an appropriate hieroglyph, and when a date was sculptured on a monument the number of periods it contained, years, months, and days, was set forth in the glyphs which denoted them. These dates can be collated with European chronology through the agency of manuscripts known as the Books of Chilan Balam, "The Tiger Priesthood," native annals of the priestly hierarchy of Yucatan, in which the entire ancient system of chronology is specifically preserved.

The annals in question were fortunately continued into the post- Conquest period, so that some of the events they date in the native manner have known European equivalents. If we count backwards from these and reduce the Maya system of computing time to the terms of our own, it becomes possible to interpret the dates on the monuments with a fair likelihood of correctness. Thus the period of the foundation of the city of Palenque has been fixed at 15 B.C.E., that of Yaxchilan at 75 B.C.E., Copan 34 C.E., Piedras Negras 109 C.E., and the abandonment of Copan and Quirigua at 231 C.E. and 292 C.E. respectively.

Perhaps no sphere of archaeology still offers such vistas of conquest as that of Central America, and the mysterious interest which cleaves to the antiquities of the isthmus is by no means yet dissipated by the searchlight of discovery. The architecture of the Maya was their greatest artistic and human triumph.

MAYAN TEMPLES AND PYRAMIDS

The wonderful structures which have aroused the admiration of generations of archaeologists, like the temples and pyramids of Egypt or the palaces of Babylon, still occupy their ancient sites and are better capable than any other manifestation of Maya life of illuminating our ideas on the subject of the civilization of Central

America. For the most part they are buried in dark and mysterious forests, although certain of them stand open on the arid plains of Yucatan, where the native genius which raised them arrived at its apogee.

The majority of these buildings were either raised for the specific purposes of religion or royal occupation. Few old domestic dwellings survive in the Maya area, these having been for the most part either constructed of adobe, or merely of reeds, like the houses of the Maya peasantry of the present day. But the greater Maya buildings were usually erected upon a mound or ku, either natural or artificial, as were some of the Mexican religious edifices.

The most general foundation of the Maya temple was a series of earth-terraces arranged in exact parallel order, the buildings themselves forming part of a square. They were constructed from the hard sandstone of the country. But the Maya were surprisingly ignorant of some of what we would call the first principles of architecture. For example, they were totally ignorant of the principles upon which the arch is constructed.

This difficulty they overcame by making each course of masonry overhang the one beneath it, after the method employed by a boy with a box of bricks, who finds that he can only make "doorways" by this means, or by the simple expedient also employed by the Maya of placing a slab horizontally upon two upright pillars. In consequence it will readily be seen that the superimposition of a second story upon such an insecure foundation was scarcely to be thought of, and that such support for the roof as towered above the doorway would necessarily require being of the most substantial description.

Indeed, this portion of the building often appears to be more than half the size of the rest of the edifice. This space gave the Maya builders a splendid chance for mural decoration, and it must be said they readily seized it and made the most of it, ornamented facades being perhaps the most typical features in the relics of Maya architecture. Apart from this, the Maya practiced a pyramidal type of architecture of which many good and even perfect examples remain. A first story was built in the usual manner, and the second rose above it by making a mound at the back of the edifice until it was on a level with the roof, and then building upon it. But length usually took the place of height in Maya architecture. Survey, design, previous calculation, all entered into the considerations of the Maya architects.

The manner in which the carved stones fitted into each other shows that they had previously been worked apart. In certain localities we discover various methods. In Chiapas we find the bas-relief in stone or stucco almost universally employed. In Honduras the stiffness of design apparent implies an older type of architecture, along with caryatids and pillars in human form.

In Guatemala there are traces of the use of wood, especially in the lintels of doorways. In the modern state of Chiapas are situated the remains of the city of Palenque, one of the most celebrated and imposing of the Maya communities, nestling on the lower slopes of the Cordilleras and built in the form of an amphitheatre. If one takes his stand on the central ku or pyramid, he finds himself surrounded by a circle of ruined palaces and temples raised upon artificial terraces.

The principal and most imposing is the Palace, a building reared upon a single platform, and in the shape of a quadrilateral surrounding a minor structure. On the walls of some of the buildings are sculptures of the Feathered Serpent, Kukulkan, or Quetzalcoatl.

The Temple of Inscriptions, perched on an eminence some 40 feet high, is the largest edifice in Palenque. It has a facade 74 feet long by 25 feet deep, composed of a great gallery which runs along the entire front of the fane.

The building has been named from the inscriptions with which certain flagstones in the central apartments are covered. Three other temples occupy a piece of rising ground close by. These are the Temple of the Sun, closely akin in type to many Japanese temple buildings; the Temple of the Cross, in which a wonderful altar-piece was discovered; and the Temple of the Cross No. II.

In the Temple of the Cross the inscribed altar gave its name to the building. In the central slab is a cross of the American pattern, its roots springing from the hideous head of the Earth-mother. Its branches stretch to where on the right and left stand two figures, evidently those of a priest and an acolyte, performing some mysterious rite.

On the apex of the tree is placed the sacred turkey, or "Emerald Fowl," to which offerings of maize paste are made. The whole is surrounded by inscriptions.

Ake, thirty miles east of Merida, is chiefly famous for its pyramids, hockey or tlachtli courts, and the gigantic pillars which once supported immense galleries. One of its principal buildings is traditionally known as "The House of Darkness," as it can boast not a single window, the light filtering in from the doorway alone.

The "Palace of Owls" is noteworthy for its diamond-shaped frieze, the work of the earliest Maya builders in Yucatan. Chichen-Itza, one of the most venerable of the ruined cities of Yucatan, is chiefly remarkable for its great pyramid-temple, known as El Castillo, which stands on a mound whence temples and palaces radiate in a circular plan.

The Temple of the Inscriptions in Palenque, Mexico. Inside the temple, two large vaulted chambers house three glyphic panels which are the second longest known inscription by the ancient Maya.

Out Of The Darkness – UFO Revelations And Planet X

Its so-called "Nunnery" is one of the most famous examples of Maya architecture, and here dwelt the sacred women, dedicated to the god Kulkucan. On the walls of the contiguous building called "El Castillo" are bas-reliefs representing Kukulkan and his priesthood. But it is impossible in a work dealing with the occult sciences of these countries to afford more than passing mention to their architecture, absorbing though it is, and we must turn to Maya history.

This commences about the beginning of the Christian era and in the area of Palenque, Piedras Negras, and Ocosingo in Chiapas. Regarding the earlier centuries we know little or nothing, and light first shines for us about the sixth century, when the Maya of Guatemala deserted their cities, and answering some unknown impulse decided to immigrate into Yucatan.

It is possible that they were forced to do so by a Nahua invasion, traces of which are to be found in a Kuikatec manuscript of early origin, but it is equally likely that, as had happened before in their history, and as is evident from the pages of *The Popol Vuh*, which supplies a precedent, that they left their settlements in the south because of some religious summons sent by the gods through their priests. But not the entire Maya race deserted their cities. Many remained, and a cleavage between the customs of the Maya of the south and those of Yucatan is hence-forward to be remarked.

Everything points to a late occupation of Yucatan by the Maya, and architectural effort exhibits deterioration, evidenced in a high conventionality of design and excess of ornamentation. Evidences of Nahua influence also are not wanting, a fact which is eloquent of the later period of contact which is known to have occurred between the peoples, and which alone is almost sufficient to fix the date of the settlement of the Maya in Yucatan.

It must not be thought that the Maya in Yucatan formed one homogeneous state recognizing a central authority. On the contrary, as is often the case with colonists, the several Maya bands of immigrants formed themselves into different states or kingdoms, each having its own separate traditions.

It is thus a matter of the greatest difficulty to so collate and criticize these traditions as to construct a history of the Maya race in Yucatan. As may be supposed, we find the various city-sites founded by divine beings that play a more or less important part in the Maya pantheon. Kukulkan, for example, is the first king of Mayapan, whilst Itzamna figures as the founder of the state of Itzamal.

The founders of the northern city of Itzamal soon formed a powerful state on a religious or priestly basis, whereas those who settled in Chichen-Itza, further to the south, were of more warlike disposition. About the year 1000 a triple alliance was entered into by Chichen-Itza, Uxmal and Mayapan, as has been said, and this lasted for about 200 years.

The people of Chichen-Itza, who were ruled by an aristocracy known as the Tutul Xius, came into conflict with the Cocomes or Nahua aristocracy of Mayapan, who, after a struggle of nearly 120 years' duration, overthrew them and made Chichen-Itza a dependency. The ruling caste, the Tutul Xius, fled southward, and settled in Potonchan, where they reigned for nearly 300 years.

They took into their service a large number of Aztec and other Nahua mercenary troops, and commenced a campaign of northward military extension, ultimately reconquering the territory they had lost to the Cocomes. Like the Romans, they made excellent roads, and wherever they made a conquest they founded a city.

This, indeed, was the period of the full blossoming of Maya art, architectural and otherwise, and from the shrines of Chichen and the island of Cozumel great highways radiated in every direction for the convenience of pilgrims. But the rule of the Mexican Cocomes still flourished and eventually became a tyranny.

The other Maya states existed in a condition of comparative servitude to them, and even the Tutul Xius had to pay a crushing tribute for the lands they held. The Cocome aristocracy, secure in its armed might, permitted itself every possible luxury and excess, morality ceased to be regarded as a virtue among them, and popular discontent was rife. The dissolute habits of the alien Cocomes at length aroused general disgust and a revolutionary feeling gained ground.

The Cocomes on their part now engaged fresh mercenaries from Mexico, and when revolt at last ensued, these stemmed the tide for some time. The Tutul Xius were forced from their possessions and settled in the city of Mani. The Cocome ruler of Mayapan, Hunac Eel, was of sterner make than his degenerate nobles.

Although tyrannical, he possessed statesmanship and experience, and resolved to attack the head and front of the rebellious states, the city of Chichen-Itza. At the head of a great host he marched against it and succeeded in inflicting a severe defeat on the Itzaes. But he had shortly to face revolution at home, and the defeated Itzaes had now joined forces with his other enemies, the Tutul Xius.

A terrific onslaught was launched against the Cocomes, and in 1436 they and their city were destroyed. They fled to Zotuta, a region in the centre of Yucatan, surrounded by almost impenetrable forests. But in crushing the Cocomes, the rulers of Chichen-Itza had almost crushed themselves.

Gradually their city crumbled into ruin, political and physical, and its aristocracy left it at last to seek the cradle of the Maya race in Guatemala, or so tradition says. The Maya people of Guatemala, the Quiches and Kakchiquels, have a separate history of their own, which is preserved for us in the pages of *The Popol Vuh*, their sacred book, a part of which the reader will find outlined in the section which deals with the arcane writings of the Maya. As with the earlier dynasties of Egypt, considerable doubt surrounds the history of the early Quiche monarchs. Indeed, a period of such uncertainty occurs that even the number of kings who reigned is lost in the hopeless confusion of varying estimates. From this chaos emerge the facts that the Quiche monarchs held the supreme power among the peoples of Guatemala, that they were the contemporaries of the rulers of Mexico City, and that they were often elected from among the princes of the subject-states.

Acxopil, the successor of Nima-Quiche, invested his second son with the government of the Kakchiquels, and placed his youngest son over the Tzutuhils, whilst to his eldest son he left the throne of the Quiches. Icutemal, his eldest son, on succeeding his father, gifted the kingdom of Kakchiquel to his eldest son, displacing his own brother and thus mortally affronting him.

The struggle which ensued lasted for generations, embittered the relations between these two branches of the Maya in Guatemala, and undermined their joint strength. Nahua mercenaries were employed in the struggle on both sides, and these introduced many of the crudities of Nahua life into Maya existence. This condition of things lasted up to the time of the coming of the Spaniards.

The Kakchiquels dated the commencement of a new chronology from the episode of the defeat of Cay Hun-Apu by them in 1492. They may have saved themselves the trouble; for the time was at hand when the calendars of their race were to be closed, and its records written in another script by another people. One by one, and chiefly by reason of their insane policy of allying themselves with the invader against their own kin, the old kingdoms of Guatemala fell as spoil to the daring Conquistadores.

Magic and divination played an extraordinary part in the policy and administration of the Maya states. No ruler would act without the advice of his soothsayers, and it may well be said that seldom has a state of fairly advanced human society acted so much in accordance with the systems and dictates of the arcane sciences.

This does not in any way imply that its downfall was due to the acceptance of such wisdom, for it was only upon the lack of observance of the mystical rule which the wise priesthood of the

Maya applied that the city-states of Yucatan crashed into ruin. Had the nobility pursued the custom of its predecessors and hearkened to the divine voices which formerly dictated their policy their fall would have been averted, but, like many another aristocracy, they forsook a well-devised theocracy for an insenate luxury and the degradations of profligate pleasure.

THE MAYA PROPHECIES

Prophecy played an important part in the lives of the Maya and occupied a prominent position in their literature. Nor was the Maya prophet without honor in his own country. Foretelling the future was the profession of a special branch of the priesthood, the members of which were called chilans. The word means mouthpiece, spokesman or interpreter, and it was the chilans who delivered to the people the responses of the gods. They were held in such high esteem that they were carried on men's shoulders when they went abroad.

The Books of Chilam Balam are the sacred books of the Maya of Yucatan and were named after their last and greatest prophet. Chilam, or chilan, was his title which means that he was the mouthpiece or interpreter of the gods. Balam means jaguar, but it is also a common family name in Yucatan, so the title of the present work could well be translated as the Book of the Prophet Balam.

During a large part of the colonial period, and even down into the Nineteenth Century, many of the towns and villages of northern Yucatan possessed Books of Chilam Balam, and this designation was supplemented by the name of the town to which the book belonged. Thus the Book of Chilam Balam of Chumayel is named for a village in the District of Tekax, a short distance northwest of the well-known town of Teabo.

This Prophet Balam lived during the last decades of the Fifteenth Century and probably the first of the Sixteenth Century and foretold the coming of strangers from the east who would establish a new religion. The prompt fulfillment of this prediction so enhanced his reputation as a seer that in later times he was considered the authority for many other prophecies which had been uttered long before his time. Inasmuch as prophecies were the most prominent feature of many of the older books of this sort, it was natural to name them after the famous soothsayer.

The Books of Chilam Balam were written in the Maya language but in the European script which the early missionaries adapted to express such sounds as were not found in Spanish. Each book is a small library in itself and contains a considerable variety of subject material. Besides the prophecies we find brief chronicles, fragmentary historical narratives, rituals, native catechisms, mythological accounts of the creation of the world, almanacs and medical treatises. Many such passages were no doubt originally transcribed from older hieroglyphic manuscripts, some of which were still in existence in northern Yucatan as late as the close of the Seventeenth Century.

As time went on, more and more European material was added to the native Maya lore. In some of the books not only do we find the ritual of a religion which is a mixture of the old faith with Christianity, but there are also translations into Maya of Spanish religious tracts and astrological treatises, as well as notes of events which occurred during the colonial period. In two of these books we even find part of a Spanish romance translated into Maya.

In the Tizimin manuscript we find an account of the manner in which Chilam Balam gave his prophecy, and it is likely that it was the customary method with this class of priests. He retired to a room in his home where he lay prostrate in a trance while the god or spirit, perched on the ridgepole of the house, spoke to the unconscious chilan below. Then the other priests assembled, probably in the reception hall of the house, and listened to the revelation with their faces bowed down to the floor.

Broadly speaking, Maya prophecies fall into four classes: day-prophecies, year-prophecies, katun-prophecies and special prophecies of the return of Quetzalcoatl, or Kukulcan as he was called by the Maya.

What we have termed the day-prophecy is more properly a prognostic, probably the business of the ah-kinyah, or diviner, rather than that of the chilan. Every one of the 260 days of the tzolkin, or tonalamatl, is specified as being lucky or unlucky, and many of them are followed by further prognostications telling whether the day is suitable for certain undertakings, lucky for certain professions and trades, auspicious for sowing certain crops, etc. These divinations are probably the scanty remnant of an extensive hieroglyphic literature exemplified by the numerous tzolkin series found in the Maya picture manuscripts. Although these almanacs are perhaps the most constant feature of the various Books of Chilam Balam, no series of this sort occurs in the Chumayel.

The predictions for the years, however, fall definitely in the field of genuine prophecy. Two versions of the series of prophecies for the twenty years of a certain Katun 5 Ahau have come down to us in the books of Tizimin and Mani. The one in the latter manuscript is entitled "Cuceb," which means squirrel, for some unknown reason.

It seems likely that these were originally the predictions corresponding to the twenty tuns of this katun, but the versions which we have, ascribed them to the Maya year, or haab, of 365 days, giving the name of the first day of each such year. As in the words of the minor Hebrew prophets, a surprisingly large proportion of the predictions are unfavorable. Drought, famine, pestilence are freely foretold, to say nothing of war, political upheavals, the sacking of towns and the captivity of the inhabitants.

Many misfortunes are symbolized by the name of the deity which brought them, and there are valuable references to religious ceremonies. The latter, coming as they do from a purely native source, are of especial importance, since practically all our knowledge of the Maya religion comes from the accounts of the Spanish missionaries who were obviously prejudiced.

Of all the prophecies, those of the katuns possess the greatest historical interest. This appears to be because whatever has occurred in the past during a certain katun is expected to recur in the future during another katun of the same name. The katun was named for the day Ahau with its numerical coefficient on which the period ended. A katun of the same name recurred after approximately 256 years, consequently at the end of that time history was expected to repeat itself. The events recounted in the Maya Chronicles found in the Mani, Tizimin and Chumayel manuscripts offer excellent grounds for believing that this belief was so strong at times as to actually influence the course of history. A surprisingly large proportion of the important upheavals in Maya history appear to have occurred in some katun named either 4 Ahau or 8 Ahau.

That the katun-prophecies written in European script in the Books of Chilam Balam correspond closely to their original form, is confirmed by the account of Father Avendaño who drew his information from the actual hieroglyphic manuscripts of the independent Itzá. The missionary's familiarity with such books and his ability to read and expound them to the Indians indicate that similar hieroglyphic manuscripts were still available for study in northern Yucatan during the last part of the Seventeenth Century, for the few days he spent at Tayasal certainly did not allow sufficient time to acquire the knowledge.

Avendaño's account explains so well the prophecies in the Books of Chilam Balam that it deserves to be given in full. It is as follows:

Out Of The Darkness – UFO Revelations And Planet X

I told them that I wished to speak to them of the old manner of reckoning which they use, both of days, months and years and of the ages, and to find out what age the present one might be (since for them one age consists only of twenty years) and what prophecy there was about the said year and age; for it is all recorded in certain books of a quarter of a yard high and about five fingers broad, made of the bark of trees, folded from one side to the other like screens; each leaf of the thickness of a Mexican Real of eight. These are painted on both sides with a variety of figures and characters (of the same kind as the Mexican Indians also used in their old times), which shows not only the count of the said days, months and years, but also the ages and prophecies which their idols and images announced to them, or, to speak more accurately, the devil by means of the worship which they pay to him in the form of some stones. These ages are thirteen in number; each age has its separate idol and its priest, with a separate prophecy of its events. These thirteen ages are divided into thirteen parts, which divide this kingdom of Yucathan and each age, with its idol, priest and prophecy, rules in one of these thirteen parts of this land, according as they have divided it; I do not give the names of the idols, priests or parts of the land, so as not to cause trouble, although I have made a treatise 1 on these old counts with all their differences and explanations, so that they may be evident to all, and the curious may learn them, for if we do not know them, I affirm that the Indians can betray us face to face.

We could hardly ask for a more accurate description of the katun-prophecies as we find them in the Books of Chilam Balam. About the only difference is that they are not written in hieroglyphics. All of them give the name of the katun, the place where it is "established" and a deity who is called "the face of the katun." The last named, however, is not described as an idol, but is said to be in the sky, or heavens. In the Chumayel and Tizimin manuscripts the prophecy is not accompanied by the name of its corresponding priest, but we find the names of these priests in the Books of Chilam Balam of Mani and Kaua. Of the prophecies themselves, more of them are unfavorable than favorable, but we do not find the complete pessimism which prevails in the year-prophecies.

Out Of The Darkness – UFO Revelations And Planet X

In the Books of Chilam Balam we find two different series of katun-prophecies, both covering the thirteen katuns which make up the "u kahlay katunob," i.e. the record of the katuns. They begin with Katun 11 Ahau, which is called the first katun because it commences with the day 1 Imix, the first day of the tzol-kin, or tonalamatl, and ends with Katun 13 Ahau. This period of thirteen katuns is the least common denominator of the 260 day tzol-kin and the katun which consists of 7200 days.

The first of these two series is evidently the older, as it takes little account of the events which occurred after the Spanish Conquest, although it does mention the actual conquest. Also its language is somewhat more symbolic than that of the other. The second series of prophecies was probably compiled at some time later than the second decade of the Seventeenth Century, judging from some of the historical allusions which it contains. Most of these allusions, however, date from before the discovery of America.

The second and later series of prophecies is completely recorded in the Chumayel, but of the first, only abbreviated versions of the prophecies for Katuns 11, 4, 2 and 13 Ahau occur. The second series is complete in the Tizimin manuscript, which also contains the prophecies of the first series. In the Books of Chilam Balam of Mani, Oxcutzcab and Kaua only the thirteen prophecies of the first series are to be found.

In both of these series of katun-prophecies the more ancient allusions are to the history of the Itzá, so far as we are able to identify them. If Avendaño was the only Spanish writer to concern himself with the katun-prophecies, such was not the case with the special prophecies which deal with the return of Quetzalcoatl. These aroused the interest of most of the early missionaries, since they were believed to foretell the coming of the Spaniards and the conversion of the Maya to Christianity.

Lizana, Cogolludo and Villagutierre all published Spanish translations of five of these, and Lizana even went so far as to quote the Maya text. To anyone who knew them only through these Spanish translations, they would appear to be inspired by missionary propaganda; but an examination of the Maya text leads to a conviction of their genuine character, in spite of the fact that any mention of the name of Quetzalcoatl has been carefully deleted.

This personage is, however, mentioned in the most obscure and guarded terms in a sixth prophecy by Chilam Balam found in the Chumayel, Tizimin and Mani manuscripts. A seventh prophecy, also ascribed to Chilam Balam, is thoroughly pagan in character, but confines its statements to predicting misfortunes of a general character in Katun 13 Ahau. Its language is archaic, and it approaches more closely the European idea of poetry than anything else found in Maya literature. Only in an eighth prophecy, ascribed to Ah Xupan Nauat, do we find a statement obviously inspired by the event itself. Here the arrival of the white men is foretold as occurring in the eighth year of Katun 13 Ahau. If Katun 13 Ahau began in 1519, this is altogether too accurate a prediction of Montejo's landing on the east coast of Yucatan in 1527 to be credited to a man said to have lived under Hun Uitzil Chac at Uxmal about the Eleventh Century C.E.

The five Maya prophets quoted by Lizana, Cogolludo and Villagutierre were Ah Kauil Chel, Napuctun, Natzin Yabun Chan, Nahau Pech and Chilam Balam It is possible that the first two were contemporaries of Ah Xupan Nauat, as the three names appear to be associated. Nothing is known of Natzin Yabun Chan to the translator. Nahau Pech is believed to have lived about four katuns, or eighty years, before the coming of the whites, which would be about the time of the fall of Mayapan. He was probably a member of the powerful Pech family which governed the Province of Ceh Pech at the time of the Conquest. The last and greatest of the Maya prophets was Chilam Balam. Balam in this case was probably the man's family name, and as among ourselves the name of his profession was prefixed to it as a title.

Chilam Balam lived at Mani during the reign of Mochan Xiu. In Katun 2 Ahau 2 he predicted that in the Katun 13 Ahau following, bearded men would come from the east and introduce a new religion. His prophecy was somewhat more definite than those of his predecessors, except for the suspicious case already mentioned. This can be accounted for by rumors of the arrival of the Spaniards in the West Indies, for we know that fishing canoes were occasionally driven across to Yucatan by storms. What Chilam Balam had in mind was the return of Quetzalcoatl and his white-robed priests, but after the Spaniards landed in Yucatan in Katun 13 Ahau according to schedule, he never ceased to be regarded as the most famous of the Maya prophets.

There are still differences in opinions when it comes to Mayan prophecies. For example, in regards to the World Age cycle that is closing in 2012 and the new World Age cycle that will begin afterwards, there are varying cosmologies as to whether we are closing the Fifth World and entering the Sixth, or closing the Fourth World and entering the Fifth.

In the perspective of the living Maya Timekeepers of Guatemala, calendrically speaking, each element has a 5,125 year cycle. They teach that we have been through fire, earth, air and water already. The next cycle (beginning Dec 21, 2012) will be ether - the Fifth Age - the Age of Center. Likewise, the Hopi teach we are closing the Fourth World of Destruction, and preparing to begin the Fifth World of Peace.

In the next chapter we will examine the theories and evidence behind Planet X, and whether or not there is any connection between the Maya prophecies and the alleged return of this mysterious planet.

CHAPTER FOUR
The Planet X/Nibiru Controversy

Astronomers have been looking for a planet at the edge of the solar system for decades. Mathematical calculations on the orbits of Jupiter, Saturn, Uranus and Neptune seemed to show that the orbital paths of these gas giants were being disturbed by another planet hiding somewhere out in the suburbs of the solar system. Using these calculations, Pluto was discovered in 1930 by Clyde Tombaugh whose job was to search though hundreds of photographs taken from the Lowell Observatory in search for Planet X.

Tombaugh's tasks was systematically to image the night sky in pairs of photographs taken two weeks apart, then examine each pair and determine whether any objects had shifted position. Using a machine called a blink comparator, he rapidly shifted back and forth between views of each of the plates, to create the illusion of movement of any objects that had changed position or appearance between photographs. On February 18, 1930, after nearly a year of searching, Tombaugh discovered a possible moving object on photographic plates taken on January 23 and January 29 of that year. A lesser-quality photograph taken on January 20 helped confirm the movement. After the observatory obtained further confirmatory photographs, news of the discovery was telegraphed to the Harvard College Observatory on March 13, 1930.

Even though Tombaugh told his bosses that he had found Planet X, it soon became clear that Pluto was too small to have any gravitational influence on its gas giant neighbors. In fact, it turns out that Pluto is so small that in 2006 it was reclassified from a planet to a dwarf planet.

Because of Pluto's size, most astronomers doubted that it could be Planet X. Throughout the mid-20th century; estimates of Pluto's mass were often revised downward. In 1978, the discovery of Pluto's moon Charon allowed the measurement of Pluto's mass for the first time. Its mass, roughly 0.2 percent that of the Earth was far too small to account for the discrepancies in Uranus; subsequent searches for an alternate Planet X failed.

Today the overwhelming consensus among astronomers is that Planet X does not exist. The early predictions had made a prediction of Planet X's position in 1915 that was fairly close to Pluto's actual position at that time; however, Ernest W. Brown concluded almost immediately that this was a coincidence, a view still held today.

There are astronomers today that still believe that Planet X could be out there somewhere. Scientists such as Kobe University astronomers Patryk Lykawka and Tadashi Mukai who announced in 2008 that computer simulations have led them to conclude it was only a matter of time before Planet X was discovered. The scientist's conclusions come from research done on the the Kuiper belt, a region at the edge of the Solar System that consists mainly of small bodies that are remnants from the Solar System's formation. The Kuiper belt objects are composed largely of frozen volatiles (dubbed "ices"), such as methane, ammonia and water. It is believed that comets originate from the Kuiper belt.

The Kuiper Belt terminates suddenly at a distance of 55 astronomical units (AU) from the Sun, and there is some speculation this sudden drop-off may be caused by the presence of an object with a mass between that of Mars and Earth located beyond 55 AU. Lykawka's and Mukai's computer simulations suggest that a body roughly the size of Earth, was ejected outward by Neptune early in the Solar System's formation and currently is in an elongated orbit between 80 and 170 AU from the Sun. Unfortunately, the majority of other astronomers view the idea of Planet X as antiquated and not worth further study.

In 1972, Joseph Brady of the Lawrence Livermore National Laboratory studied irregularities in the motion of Halley's Comet. Brady claimed that they could have been caused by a Jupiter-sized planet beyond Neptune that orbited the Sun backward. As well, in the 1980s and 1990s, astronomer Robert Sutton Harrington of the U.S. Naval Observatory, who had first calculated that Pluto was too small to have perturbed the orbits of Uranus and Neptune, led a search to determine the real cause of the planets' apparently irregular orbits. He calculated that any Planet X would be at roughly three times the distance from the sun of Neptune's orbit, highly elliptical, and far below the ecliptic (the planet's orbit would be at roughly a 90-degree angle from the orbital plane of the other known planets).

Another theory proposed in 1999 by John Murray of the Open University and John Matese, Patrick Whitman and Daniel Whitmire of the University of Louisiana at Lafayette, has long period comets originating from specific regions of the sky, rather than coming from random directions as proposed by Oort. This would result from comets being disturbed by an unseen object at least as large as Jupiter, and possibly a brown dwarf.

So while many astronomers dismiss the idea of Planet X, there are those who feel that it is still worth conducting deep-space research in order to try to solve the mystery once and for all. These astronomers, unfortunately, are in the minority.

THE SEARCH FOR OTHER PLANETS

Over the centuries astronomers believed that there were other mysterious planets in our solar system that like Planet X, were just waiting to be discovered. The French mathematician Urbain Le Verrier, during a lecture on January 2, 1860, announced that the problem of observed deviations of the motion of Mercury could be solved by assuming an intra-Mercurial planet, or possibly a second asteroid belt inside Mercury's orbit. The only possible way to observe this intra-Mercurial planet or asteroids was if/when they transited the Sun, or during total solar eclipses.

Prof. Wolf at the Zurich sunspot data center, found a number of suspicious "dots" on the Sun, and another astronomer found some more. A total of two dozen spots seemed to fit the pattern of two intra-Mercurial orbits, one with a period of 26 days and the other of 38 days.

In 1859, Le Verrier received a letter from the amateur astronomer Lescarbault, who reported having seen a round black spot on the Sun on March 26, 1859, looking like a planet transiting the Sun. He had seen the spot one hour and a quarter, when it moved a quarter of the solar diameter, and its total transit time across the solar disk was four hours 30 minutes.

Le Verrier investigated this observation, and computed an orbit of 19 days 7 hours. The diameter was considerably smaller than Mercury's and its mass was estimated at 1/17 of Mercury's mass. This was too small to account for the deviations of Mercury's orbit, but perhaps this was the largest member of that intra-Mercurial asteroid belt. Le Verrier named the planet, Vulcan.

In 1860 there was a total eclipse of the Sun and Le Verrier mobilized all French and some other astronomers to find Vulcan. However, it failed to make an appearance.

On April 4 1875, a German astronomer, H. Weber, saw a round spot on the Sun. Le Verrier's orbit indicated a possible transit at April 3 that year, and Wolf noticed that his 38-day orbit also could have performed a transit at about that time. That "round dot" was also photographed at Greenwich and in Madrid.

Vulcan continued to be spotted by astronomers over the next several years. During the total solar eclipse on July 29, 1878, two observers claimed to have seen in the vicinity of the Sun small illuminated disks which could only be small planets inside Mercury's orbit: J.C Watson (professor of astronomy at the Univ. of Michigan) believed he'd found two intra-Mercurial planets. Lewis Swift (co-discoverer of Comet Swift-Tuttle, which returned 1992), also saw a "star" he believed to be Vulcan, but at a different position than either of Watson's two intra-Mercurials.

After this, Vulcan was never spotted again. Just what exactly Lescarbault and other astronomers had seen remain a mystery. It is possible that they had happened to see a small asteroid passing very close to the Earth. Such asteroids were unknown at that time, but it is doubtful that the telescopes of that period would have been able to discern a small asteroid that close to the Earth.

Vulcan was briefly revived around 1970-1971, when a few researchers thought they had detected several faint objects close to the Sun during a total solar eclipse. Again, there have been no good explanations on just what these astronomers had seen. So it does seem that the solar system does have a few surprises waiting to be uncovered.

NEITH, THE MOON OF VENUS

In 1672, Giovanni Domenico Cassini, one of the prominent astronomers of the time, noticed a small companion, possibly a moon, close to Venus. Cassini decided not to announce his observation, but 14 years later, in 1686, he saw the object again, and then entered it in his journal.

The object was estimated to have about 1/4 the diameter of Venus, and it showed the same phase as Venus. Later, the object was seen by other astronomers as well: by James Short in 1740, Andreas Mayer in 1759, J. L. Lagrange in 1761 (Lagrange announced that the orbital plane of the satellite was perpendicular to the ecliptic).

During 1761 the object was seen a total of 18 times by five observers. The observations of Scheuten on June 6, 1761 was especially interesting: he saw Venus in transit across the Sun's disk, accompanied by a smaller dark spot on one side, which followed Venus in its transit. However, Samuel Dunn at Chelsea, England, who also watched that transit, did not see that additional spot. In

1764 there were eight observations by two observers. Other observers tried to see the satellite but failed to find it.

In 1766, Father Hell, the director of the Vienna observatory, published a treatise where he declared that all observations of the satellite were optical illusions. Hell explained that the image of Venus is so bright that it is reflected in the eye, back into the telescope, creating a secondary image at a smaller scale.

Others published treatises declared that the observations were real and J. H. Lambert of Germany published orbital elements of the satellite in *Berliner Astronomischer Jahrbuch 1777*. It was hoped that the satellite could be seen during the transit of Venus in front of the Sun on June 1, 1777, but nothing was seen.

In 1768 there was another observation of the satellite, by Christian Horrebow in Copenhagen. In 1884, M. Hozeau, former director of the Royal Observatory of Brussels, suggested that by analyzing available observations, the Venus moon appeared close to Venus approximately every 2.96 years or 1080 days. Hozeau suggested that it wasn't a moon of Venus, but a planet of its own, orbiting the sun once every 283 days and thus being in conjunction with Venus once every 1080 days. Hozeau also named it NEITH, after the mysterious goddess of Sais, whose veil no mortal raised.

By the 19th century, most astronomers had dismissed sightings of Neith as mistakes involving stars. But on Aug 13, 1892 E. E. Barnard recorded a 7th magnitude object near Venus. There is no star in the position recorded by Barnard, and Barnard's eyesight was notoriously excellent, so there is one more celestial mystery that we can add to that big bag of surprises lorded over us by the solar system.

NEMESIS, THE SUN'S COMPANION STAR

It started as a discussion in 1983 between two experimental physicists, Richard Muller and Luis Alvarez, regarding a paper they had received. The paper came from David Raup and John Sepkoski, two respected paleontologists, and they were making the remarkable claim that great catastrophes occur on the Earth every 26 million years, like clockwork. It was only 4 years earlier in 1979 that Alvarez had proposed that the extinction of the dinosaurs had been triggered 65 million years ago by an asteroid crashing into the Earth.

Many paleontologists had initially paid no regard to this theory, and one had publicly dismissed Alvarez as a 'nut', regardless of his Nobel Prize in physics. But David Raup and John Sepkoski had both liked Alvarez's asteroid theory and now were sending their own theory to Alvarez, or rather their findings, as they offered no explanation. Muller and Alvarez agreed to research their bizarre claim that great catastrophes occur on the Earth every 26 million years.

Raup and Sepkoski had collected a vast amount of data on family extinctions in the oceans, far more than had previously been assembled, and their analysis showed that there were intense periods of extinctions every 26 million years. It wasn't surprising that there should be extinctions this often, but it was surprising that they should be so regularly spaced.

Alvarez's work had already shown that at least two of these extinctions were caused by asteroid impacts, the one that killed the dinosaurs at the end of the Cretaceous period, 65 million years ago, and one that killed many land mammals at the end of the Eocene, 35-39 million years ago. But these new findings beggared belief, what could be the cause of such regular events? Was it credible that an asteroid would hit the Earth every 26 million years?

An asteroid passing close to the sun has only slightly better than one chance in a billion of hitting our planet. The impacts that do occur should be randomly spaced, not hitting us at precise intervals of every 26 million years. What could make them hit on such a regular schedule? It was ludicrous, but physicists have a wry saying: "If it happens, then it must be possible."

Muller replotted the data using the conventions of physicists rather than paleontologists, giving each extinction an uncertainty in age as well as in intensity. He then placed arrows at regular 26 million year intervals. Eight of them pointed right at the extinction peaks, only two missed. The new chart was more impressive than Muller had expected.

The figures looked impressive, there were mass extinctions every 26 million years, two of them were known to be caused as a result of asteroid impacts, but could they all be? What could cause it? What model could they come up with to explain it?

Alvarez challenged Muller to come up with a model, and Muller duly obliged: "Suppose there is a companion star that orbits the sun. Every 26 million years it comes close to the Earth and does something, I'm not sure what, but it makes asteroids hit the Earth. Maybe it brings the asteroids with it."

Alvarez agreed it was possible, and they carried out calculations to see if the orbit of a companion star was possible without being so big that it would be carried away by the gravity of other nearby stars. The major diameter of an elliptical orbit is the period of the orbit, in this case 26 million years, raised to the 2/3 power, and multiplied by two. Muller quickly showed this to be about 2.8 light years. That put the companion star close enough to the sun so it would not get pulled away by other stars. Alvarez agreed – the model was holding up. The hypothetical star was named "Nemesis."

It was proposed that Nemesis, in passing through the Oort cloud, would perturb the orbit of some of the comets and send them towards the inner parts of the solar system and towards our planet. It is believed to be a dark star, a large mass, much larger than a planet, but not large enough to form a bright star, probably a red or brown dwarf (a planet-like body insufficiently massive to start burning hydrogen like a star). It is possible that this star already exists in one of the catalogs of dim stars without anyone having noted something peculiar, namely the enormous apparent motion of that star against the background of more distant stars.

The probability of a companion star also gains support by the fact that more than 50% of stars in a galaxy are in a binary system, which would lead one to conclude that a "death" companion star to the sun to be a probable reality. The search for Nemesis is currently underway at the Leuschner Observatory in Layfette, California with an automated telescope. To determine which star is the Sun's companion star, photographs of 5,000 red stars have been taken along with the measurement of the apparent shift in position determined by a second photograph picture taken two to six months later. A small change in position indicates that the stars are far away. Stars that are close enough to possibly be Nemesis will show a significant shift in position. It is thought that Nemesis, if it exists, will be discovered in the Hydra constellation.

NIBIRU AND THE WORKS OF ZECHARIAH SITCHIN

This now brings us to the amazing theories of Zechariah Sitchin, which are based on his translations of ancient Sumerian cuneiforms. In 1976, Sitchin published the book *The 12th Planet* in which he proposed, based on his translations of Sumerian myths and legends, of a planet with a comet-like orbit that came into our area of the solar system every 3,600 years.

In his book, Sitchin writes that there is one more planet in our solar system and it comes between Mars and Jupiter every 3,600 years. People from that planet came to Earth almost half a million years ago and did many of the things about which we read in the book of Genesis. This planet is inhabited by intelligent human beings who created Homo sapiens. "We look like them," says Sitchin. "I call them the Annunaki."

The starting point for Sitchin's research goes back to his childhood when he would wonder about the Nefilim, who are mentioned in Genesis, Chapter six, as the sons of the gods who married the daughters of Man in the days before the great flood. The word Nefilim is commonly translated as giants; "There were the days when there were giants upon the Earth."

Sitchin felt that this interpretation seemed inaccurate because the word Nefilim literally means: "Those who have come down to Earth from the heavens." In order to get a better understanding, Sitchin focused on Sumer and learned to read the cuneiform Sumerian texts. This was because all the ancient scriptures, the Bible, the Greek myths, the Egyptian myths and texts, had their roots originating from the 6,000 year-old Sumerian civilization.

What Sitchin discovered took him completely by surprise as he came upon the Sumerians persistent and repeated statements that those beings, which were called Anunnaki, came to Earth from a planet called Nibiru.

In the cuneiforms, Nibiru is designated by the sign of the cross which meant "planet of crossing." Sitchin then shifted his research from who were the Nefilim and the Anunnaki, to astronomy to try and learn what planet the Sumerians were referring to.

Scholars were undecided on what planet was supposed to be Nibiru. Some said it was Mars, which was described and known to the ancient people. Others said it was Jupiter. Sitchin decided that they all were wrong because the cuneiform scripts description of Nibiru and its position when it nears the Sun indicated that it could not be Mars, and it could not be Jupiter. This could only mean that it is one more planet that comes periodically between Mars and Jupiter; it is sometimes nearer to Mars and sometimes nearer to Jupiter.

Once Sitchin realized that this was the answer, that there is another, unknown planet, everything fell into place. This explained the meaning of the Mesopotamian Epic of Creation on which the first chapters of Genesis are based, and all details about the Anunnaki, who they were and who their leaders were, became crystal clear.

The Sumerians wrote that their great knowledge "was told to us by the Anunnaki." They knew about and described the planets Uranus, Neptune and Pluto. They were proficient in mathematics and, in many respects, their knowledge surpassed modern times.

Sitchin says that the existence of Nibiru is not a matter of just one more planet in our solar system. If Nibiru exists, and the Anunnaki exist, then the Sumerian claim that they come back to our vicinity every 3,600 years, then we are not alone and there are more advanced people than us in our solar system.

People from Nibiru came to Earth almost half a million years ago who created Homo sapiens. "We look like them," says Zechariah Sitchin. "I call them the Annunaki."

This unknown planet was also known by other ancient societies. Between the Babylonians and Mesopotamians there were at least three names: "Marduk," "The King of The Heavens," and the "Great Heavenly Body." The ancient Hebrews referred to it as the "Winged Globe" because of its long orbit high among the stars. The Egyptians had two names "Apep" or "Seth." The Greeks called it "Typhon" after a feared leader and "Nemesis." Other ancient peoples have given it labels such as; "The Celestial Lord Shiva" and "God of Destruction." To the ancient Chinese, it was known as "Gung-gung," "The Great Black," or "Red Dragon." The Phoenicians said it was "The Great Phoenix." The Maya called it "Celestial Quetzalcoatl." The celestial body was known to the Romans as "Lucifer" and "Wormwood."

The "Red or Blue Star" is from the Hopi Indian. The "Fiery Messenger" is in the Ramala prophecy. The "Great Star" is from the Book Revelation. "His Star" is how it is referred to in Edgar Cayce Readings. The "Great Comet" and "The Comet of Doom" is right out of the Grail Message. The early English prophet Mother Shipton called it "The Fiery Dragon." The Kolbrin Bible refers to it as "Destroyer."

THE ORIGINS OF MANKIND

One of Sitchin's most controversial theories (among many), is his thesis that mankind is not a product of either Biblical creation, or of evolution. Instead, Sitchin says that humanity was a genetic product of the extraterrestrial Anunnaki for the soul purpose of being slave labor.

The Annunnaki, or Nephlim, landed on Earth over 400,000 years ago and colonized it. They established a spaceport in what today is the Iraq-Iran area, and lived in a kind of idealistic society as a small colony. Their purpose here was to mine for gold and other minerals. However, is there any proof that mankind is the creation of beings from another world?

Sitchin notes that Man's ancestor apes existed 25 million years ago; it took 11 million years for a manlike ape to appear and then it was another 11 million years until the first ape-man worthy of the classification Homo appeared. The first being considered truly manlike was Advanced Australopithecus some two million years ago.

It took another million years for Homo erectus to appear and yet another million for Neanderthal man to arrive — and he looked much like Australopithecus and used almost identical tools. Then about 35 thousand years ago Homo sapiens suddenly appeared in the form of Cro-Magnon man with specialized tools, the ability to build shelters and art forms that reflected organized society and a rudimentary culture. A few thousand years later the high civilizations of Mesopotamia appeared. And in the blink of an eye, humans were traveling in space, involved in genetic engineering and threatening their own planet. Furthermore, more recent discoveries revealed that Homo sapiens other than Cro-Magnon predated Neanderthal man by some 200 thousand years and appeared during an ice age, a period assumed to be unsuited for rapid evolution. Thus, a more advanced species inexplicably appeared prior to a less evolved one. This draws into question the idea of slow, steady, progressive evolution. Clearly, there were (and are) large things unexplained by evolution alone.

Sitchin's analysis draws heavily from the Mesopotamian scholarship that has been undertaken over the last century. However, Sitchin, who was born in Russia and raised in Palestine, draws upon his own deep knowledge of ancient and modern Middle Eastern languages to challenge the current linguistic interpretation of Mesopotamian terminology, which in many cases Sitchin considers a result of pre-formed conclusions about the alleged impossibility of what these texts seemingly assert.

Sitchin brings God's creation of Man into the picture by using ancient texts that indicate the use of genetic engineering to accelerate the development of ape-like creatures on Earth, to work in the gold mines that the Anunnaki had established in southern Africa. In the process, he finds in the texts evidence of failed attempts to genetically create modern humans that produced mutants which may well have served as the models of the animal-human forms that abound in Greek mythology.

Ancient Mesopotamian tablets credit one "god" in particular with supervising the genetic manufacture of Homo sapiens. That "god's" name was Ea. Ea was the son of Anu, who was the ruler of another world. Prince Ea was known by the title, "EN.KI," which means "Lord [or Prince] of Earth."

Mesopotamian texts portray Prince Ea as an advocate who spoke before the council of the gods on behalf of the new earth race. Ea opposed many of the cruelties that other "gods," including his half brother, Enlil, inflicted upon human beings. When the idea of creating a primitive worker made it to the council of the gods, they wondered how a being intelligent enough to use tools and to follow orders could be created. A Sumerian text has immortalized the answer given by EA to the assembled Anunnaki, who saw in the creation of an Adamu the solution to their unbearable toil: "The creature whose name you uttered – IT EXISTS! All you have to do, he added, is to Bind upon it the image of the gods."

Out Of The Darkness – UFO Revelations And Planet X

The process envisioned by EA was to "bind" upon the existing apeman/apewoman through genetic manipulation. In other words, they combined their genes with that of the Neanderthals, upgrading Neanderthals to human beings. The term Adamu, which is clearly the inspiration for the biblical name Adam, and the use of the term "image" in Sumerian text, which is repeated intact in the biblical text, are not the only clues to the Sumerian/Mesopotamian origin of the Genesis creation of Mankind. The biblical use of the plural pronoun and the depiction of a group of Elohim reaching a consensus and following it up with the necessary action also lose their enigmatic aspects when the Mesopotamian sources are taken into account.

The verse, "God said, Let us make men in our image, after our likeness" reveals not only God in the plural but it also reflects that we humans are genetically connected to the Elohim. After EA created the human race he wanted to teach humanity truth in spirituality. But the other Anunnaki wanted to remain in control of the Adam. EA formed an organization called "The Brotherhood of the Serpent/Snake." Its original purpose was to educate the human race in spiritual truth.

The other "gods" didn't want the human race to be free, all they wanted was to control the human race. So they taught falsehoods regarding Prince Ea. They taught that Ea was evil, calling him Satan, Prince of Darkness, evil incarnate etc. The truth of the matter is that Ea was against the harsh treatment of the human race, he was the true friend of human beings.

This puts the book of Genesis and the fall of Adam and Eve into an entirely different perspective. God in the Bible wants to keep knowledge away from humanity, but the serpent, the true friend of Man, knows that their creation deserves to learn about its spiritual heritage.

After Mankind ate of the fruit (learned knowledge), they knew they were naked. This reminded them of their slavery to the "gods," something that was extremely unpleasant. The Anunnaki clearly did not want the human race to recover spiritually. The reason, they wanted slaves. Humans do the work, while these "gods" live in the lap of luxury. Therefore the Lord God sent him (Adam) forth from the Garden of Eden, to till the ground from which he had been taken. So he drove out the man; and he placed at the east of the Garden of Eden cherubim (angels), and a flaming sword which turned every way, to shield the way to the tree of life. Genesis 3:23-24

Right after Mankind ate of the fruit he was cast out of "paradise," cast out of Eden. The "flaming sword" symbolizes the no-nonsense measures that the gods undertook to ensure that genuine spiritual knowledge would never become available to the human race.

To further prevent access to such knowledge, Homo Sapiens were condemned to an additional fate: "And to Adam, he (God) said, Because you have listened to the urgings of your wife, and have eaten from the tree of which I commanded you not to, saying, You shall not partake of it: cursed is the ground for you, in toil will you eat its yield for all the days of your life: Thorns, too, and thistles will it bring forth to you; as you eat the plants from the field. By the sweat of your face will you eat bread, until you return to the ground; for out of it were you taken: for dust you are and to dust will you return." Genesis 3:17-19

The above passage reflects that the Anunnaki never intended humans to rise above the level of material existence. It would leave little time for humans to seek out the understanding they needed to become spiritually free. Humans have been deliberately misled about their true spirituality. Religion, as introduced to mankind by the Anunnaki, is meant to keep us ignorant and subservient. Follow the laws of God, do not ask questions, and seek not knowledge, for you shall surely die. This is the teachings and the way of a master over his slaves. We were born as slaves, and the "gods" intend for us to die as slaves.

Michael Tellinger in his article *Chromosome Fusion: Evidence of DNA manipulation in our distant past?* writes that the Human Genome Project presented some mysteries for scientists who had no explanation on why the vast percentage of the human DNA is inactive. It is estimated that at least 97% of our DNA is a waste of space, as it does not contain any active genes that actually carry the code for any of our physical makeup. Then within the genes there are Introns – parts that do not carry any code; and Exons - sections that carry some sort of genetic code. The full length of our DNA is made up of some 20 000 genes that have now been identified. These genes carry the blueprint for the structure of our entire body. What is very puzzling is the fact that Homo sapiens, as the supposed pinnacle if civilized evolution on this planet, should have such large parts of unused DNA. We seem to have the longest DNA molecule among all other species, but we use the smallest part of it in proportion to the other species. In other words, all the other creatures use much more of their DNA than humans do. Some species use as much as 98% of their DNA.

This flies directly in the face of the principles of evolution. Humans should have the most complex and evolved DNA of all creatures, to have reached levels of civilization seemingly much higher than any other species on Earth over millions of years of evolution. What is even more curious is the predicted number of genes in species. The numbers seem to increase steadily from basic organisms to the most advanced. We would expect that humans should end up having most genes, but strangely this is not the case.

Here are some examples of the predictions for total number of genes in species.

Fruit Fly	21,000
Zebrafish	50,000
Chicken	76,000
Mouse	81,000
Chimp	130,000
Human	68,000

The Chimp is our closest genetic relative and yet it has almost twice as many genes as humans. And then we get to the anomaly of the chromosomes. Our DNA is broken up into 23 pairs of chromosomes. By comparison, all apes have 24 pairs. One would expect that Homo erectus, our immediate evolutionary precursor would then also have had 24 chromosome pairs.

On April 6, 2005, researchers from the National Human Genome Research Institute announced that, "A detailed analysis of chromosomes 2 and 4 has detected the largest 'gene deserts' known in the human genome and uncovered more evidence that human chromosome 2 arose from the fusion of two ancestral ape chromosomes."

So when we read in the Sumerian tablets that humans were cloned as a sub-species between Homo erectus and a more advanced human-like species that arrived on Earth some 400,000 years ago, it suddenly makes a little bit more sense. The tablets describe how our maker removed certain parts of the "Tree of life" to trim the ability of the new "creature" and how they struggled to make the perfect "primitive worker" so that it could understand commands but not be too smart to question their existence. Similar suggestions of genetic cloning are made in The Koran and Hindu Laws of Manu.

The Koran: · *Ya Sin: "Is man not aware that We created him from a little germ?"*

The Believers - *God says almost verbatim what the Sumerian tablets tell us. "We first created man from an essence of* *clay; then placed him a living germ in a secure enclosure. The germ we made a clot of blood, and the clot a lump of flesh. This we fashioned into bones, then clothed the bones with flesh..."*

Laws of Manu: *· 19. But from minute body (-framing) particles of these seven very powerful Purushas springs this (world), the perishable from the imperishable. · 20. Among them each succeeding (element) acquires the quality of the preceding one, and whatever place (in the sequence) each of them occupies, even so many qualities it is declared to possess.*

THE CREATION OF THE SOLAR SYSTEM

The Sumerians scientific knowledge, especially their understanding of the solar system, seems to defy current scientific theories on the development of some ancient civilizations. Zechariah Sitchin, during his research, decided to take a radically different interpretation of the clay cuneiforms. Where previously scientists regarded the Sumerian writings as simply myths and legends, Sitchin took the stance of "what if" and considered that these stories could be true accounts of ancient oral histories that had been handed down from generation to generation before finally being committed to clay.

This is not to say that everything written on the tablets were to be thought of as totally factual. Sitchin understood that there were differences between what were obviously religious and social myths, fairytales so to speak, and writings that were considered historical, science-based, and current events. When these writings were given a second look, Sitchin was astonished to find a vast storehouse of knowledge that seemed completely out of place with such an ancient civilization.

According to Sitchin's interpretation of a book called *The Creation Epic*, the Sumerians believed that about four billion years ago, the Earth, as we know it did not exist. If we were to name the planets, starting from the Sun, we would have Mercury (Mummu), Venus (Lahamu), Mars (Lahmu), Tiamat, Kingu, Jupiter (Kishar), Saturn (Anshar), Uranus (Anu), Neptune (Ea), and Pluto (Gaga).

The first words of The Creation Epic, given to Gilgamesh, were, Enuma Elish, "When in the heights," which basically is the same as in the opening of Genesis "In the beginning..." Scholars now know that the first few chapters of Genesis are really a condensed version of Enuma Elish.

In the beginning, a planet, about four times the size of planet Earth broke away from another star system in deep space which eventually brought it close to our solar system. The name of this planet was Nibiru. It brought with it four moons known as "Winds," the North Wind, the East Wind, the South Wind, and the West Wind.

Our solar system drew Nibiru closer and closer because of gravitational forces, until it was finally captured in an eccentric orbit that takes it into deep space and then back again around the Sun. Nibiru, unlike the other planets, has a clockwise orbit that brings it into the solar system between Mars and Jupiter.

As Nibiru entered the solar system, it encountered a planet (about twice the size of Earth) orbiting between Mars and Jupiter. This planet was called Tiamat by the Sumerians (Teom, by the later Hebrews). Tiamat had many small moons and one large moon named Kingu. Kingu was in the process of becoming a full planet in its own right, when Nibiru and its moons arrived.

The ancient text describes a monumental battle of the gods as Nibiru swung in on an arc that put it on a collision course with Tiamat. At that moment, Kingu (Tiamat's large moon) came between Nibiru and Tiamat. One of the Winds (moons) of Nibiru swung into position in front of Nibiru to do battle with Kingu. Kingu took the first hit as Nibiru's moon struck, and glanced off of Kingu.

This brought Nibiru's moon into a position where it was heading straight for Tiamat. Tiamat sent out incredible bolts of lightning toward Nibiru's moon, but to no avail...the moon of Nibiru struck the mighty dragon Tiamat and cracked it like an egg, leaving it to writhe in pain, its life all but extinguished.

Nibiru passed Tiamat on its first orbit through the solar system, moving around the sun and out into deep space. Thirty six hundred years later, it returned with a vengeance. Nibiru this time struck Tiamat head on, pulverizing half of the doomed planet.

The Winds (moons) of Nibiru fought with the remaining moons of Tiamat, sending them off into space, to return periodically as meteors. Half of Tiamat, along with its now dead moon Kingu, was hurled into a new orbit between Venus and Mars. So according to the Sumerians, the Earth was originally part of a much larger planet that was blasted into oblivion by Planet X, and the dead Kingu is now our Moon.

Nibiru's orbit stabilized after its confrontation with Tiamat/Earth. Every 3,600 years it makes its long journey (in a clockwise direction) around our Sun and through the space between Mars and Jupiter.

If this is indeed the case—that Nibiru reenters the solar system every 3,600 years, there should be some historical evidence that this celestial phenomenon does take place. As well, depending on where the Earth (as well as Mars and Jupiter) is positioned in its orbit around the sun, when Nibiru comes up through the solar system its mass and gravity is almost certain to cause major disruptions upon nearby planets, and possibly even the entire solar system.

Is there any evidence that at specific times in the past, there were major environmental catastrophes such as floods, earthquakes, volcanoes, horrific windstorms etc.? A Russian-born doctor by the name of Immanuel Velikovsky wondered the very same thing, and after years of research, published a series of books that even today generates considerable controversy within the scientific community.

Art By Carol Rodriguez

CHAPTER FIVE
The Suppression of Immanuel Velikovsky
By Tim R. Swartz

In reading Zechariah Sitchin's interpretation of the Sumerian *Creation Epic*, with its tales of great planets wheeling in bloody battle through the lightning emblazoned sky, we are left with a feeling that we may have heard this type of story before. Practically every civilization that has popped up out of the dust has their ancient tales of mythical conquests, epic adventures, and cataclysmic events. Modern science dismisses these stories as simple fairy tales and folklore meant for entertainment on those cold nights around the fire. Yet, close examinations of these narratives, which came from cultures that were continents apart, show some interesting and downright perplexing similarities.

Immanuel Velikovsky, born in Vitebsk, Russia in 1895, never intended to create the storm of academic controversy that resulted in the publication of his book *Worlds in Collision*. His original intention was to write a book about Sigmund Freud's dream interpretation with a new view of Freud's hero's Oedipus and Akhnaton. For research purposes, Velikovsky needed access to numerous literary sources. For this reason, in 1939 he traveled from his home in Palestine to New York along with his family. Unfortunately, shortly after arriving in the U.S. WW II began and Velikovsky and his family became permanent residents of the U.S.

As Velikovsky conducted research for *Oedipus & Akhnaton*, he got deeply involved in the study of ancient history, the Near East in particular. Velikovsky wondered about the catastrophes said to have accompanied the Hebrew Exodus, when fire and hailstones rained upon Egypt, earthquakes decimated the nation, and a pillar of fire and smoke moved in the sky. Biblical and other traditional Hebrew sources speak so vividly that Velikovsky began to speculate if some extraordinary natural event might have played a part in the Exodus.

Out Of The Darkness – UFO Revelations And Planet X

To explore this possibility, Velikovsky sought out a corresponding account in ancient Egyptian records, finding a remarkable parallel in a papyrus kept at the University of Leyden Museum, called the Papyrus Ipuwer. The document contains the lamentations of an Egyptian sage in response to a great catastrophe overwhelming Egypt, when the rivers ran red, fire blazed in the sky, and pestilence ravaged the land.

Velikovsky also encountered surprising parallels in Babylonian and Assyrian clay tablets, Vedic poems, Chinese epics, and North American Indian, Maya, Aztec, and Peruvian legends. From these remarkably similar accounts, he constructed a thesis of celestial catastrophe. He concluded that a very large body – apparently a "comet" – passed close enough to Earth to violently perturb its axis, as global earthquakes, wind and falling stone decimated early civilizations.

Before Velikovsky could complete his reconstruction, he had to resolve an enigma. He had found that in the accounts of far-flung cultures, the cometary agent of disaster was identified as a planet. And the closer he looked, the more clear it became to him that this planet was Venus: The converging ancient images include the Babylonian "torch-star" Venus and "bearded star" Venus, the Mexican "smoking star" Venus, the Peruvian "long-haired" star Venus, the Egyptian Great Star "scattering its flame in fire" and the widespread imagery of Venus as a flaming serpent or dragon in the sky. In each instance, the cometary language is undeniable, for these were the very symbols of "the comet" in the ancient languages.

By following the evidence, Velikovsky discovered that Venus holds a special place among the planet's first astronomers. In both the Old World and the New, ancient stargazers regarded Venus with awe and terror, carefully observing its risings and settings, and claiming the planet to be the cause of world-ending catastrophe. These astronomical traditions, Velikovsky reasoned, must have had roots in a traumatic human experience, though modern science has always assumed that the planets evolved in quiet and undisturbed isolation over billions of years.

Intrigued, Velikovsky studied ancient sources from all cultures around the planet in a meticulous 10-year research project. Everywhere he looked, Velikovsky found similar stories about great natural catastrophes. He could only come to the conclusion that at certain times in the far past, there must have been dramatic, catastrophic events that encompassed the entire globe.

This was in clear contradiction to the widely-accepted theory of uniformity. This geological theory says the state of the Earth today is a result of a series of minute changes over very long periods of time. Uniformity says that if the solar system is quiet now, then it was also quiet in the past. Even more surprising, Velikovsky discovered that the dates of these Earth-shaking catastrophes would have put them within historical times, when according to accepted historical and geological knowledge, everything was quiet and normal.

As well, Velikovsky discovered that the generally accepted chronology of the history of Ancient Egypt was wrong by several centuries. In detailed research, he reconstructed the actual course of events and could find a simple and straightforward solution to many known inconsistencies. In order to verify his findings from the study of ancient sources, Velikovsky also comprehensively dealt with geological, palaeontological and archaeological facts, which strangely enough from the point of view of the accepted teachings led to similar conclusions.

The unique feature of Velikovsky's approach was that he didn't try to interpret the traditional human testimony, or to understand it in a metaphorical sense, but that he took it as literally as it had been written down. This approach led him to an even more far-reaching conclusion about the cause of the described catastrophes.

According to Velikovsky, the planets Venus and Mars, despite their modern status as stable worlds, played a crucial role in past, catastrophic natural events. The mythological and historical traditions of our ancestors described events in the sky that turn our entire concepts of the origin and history of our planetary system upside down.

Velikovsky was well aware of the importance of his conclusions and only published elements that he could definitely prove, often by several independent sources. However, he had little idea that his book would create the controversy that it did. *Worlds in Collision* caused an outcry among scientists and the public alike that had not been seen in the history of science since the days of Galileo.

WORLDS IN COLLISION

Worlds in Collision was published by Macmillan, who had a large presence in the academic textbook market. Even before its release, the book was drawn into controversy when *Harper's Magazine* published a highly positive feature on it. This came to the attention of astronomer Harlow Shapley, who threatened to organize a textbook boycott of Macmillan. Within two months the book was transferred to Doubleday, but by then it was already a best seller.

Immanuel Velikovsky in his book *Worlds in Collision* proposes that many myths and traditions of ancient peoples and cultures are based on actual events: worldwide global catastrophes of a celestial origin, which had a profound effect on the lives, beliefs and writings of early mankind.

Out Of The Darkness – UFO Revelations And Planet X

Worlds in Collision deals in particular with two catastrophes: the first one associated with Exodus, the second one with the siege of Jerusalem by Sennacherib. The book proposed that around the 15th century B.C.E., a comet or comet-like object (now called the planet Venus), having originally been ejected from Jupiter, passed near Earth (an actual collision is not mentioned). The object changed Earth's orbit and axis, causing numerous catastrophes which were mentioned in early mythologies and religions around the world.

Fifty-two years later, the comet passed by once again, stopping the Earth's rotation and causing more destruction. Then, in the 8th and 7th centuries B.C.E., Mars (itself displaced by Venus) made close approaches to the Earth; this incident caused a new round of disturbances and disasters. After that, the current "celestial order" was established and the courses of the planets stabilized over the centuries with Venus gradually becoming a "normal" planet. To explain the celestial mechanics necessary to permit these changes to the configuration of the solar system, Velikovsky thought that electromagnetic forces might somehow play a greater role to counteract gravity and orbital mechanics.

Velikovsky argued that the terrifying "gods" of the ancient world were planets, and he recounts two close encounters of the comet or protoplanet Venus with the Earth. Included in the same volume was a large section on the ancient war god, whom Velikovsky identified as the planet Mars. He claimed that for hundreds of years after the Venus catastrophes, Mars moved on an unstable orbit intersecting that of Earth, leading to a series of Earth-disturbing events in the eighth and seventh centuries B.CE.

One problem that faced Velikovsky was the apparent differences in the recorded dates that his theorized catastrophes occurred. He argued that the conventional chronology of the Near East and classical world, based upon Egyptian Sothic dating and the king lists of Manetho, was flawed. This was the reason for the apparent absence of correlation between the Biblical record and those of neighboring cultures, and also the cause of the enigmatic "Dark Ages" in Greece and elsewhere.

Velikovsky shifted several chronologies and dynasties from the Egyptian Old Kingdom to Ptolemaic times by centuries (a scheme he called the Revised Chronology), placing the Exodus contemporary with the fall of the Middle Kingdom of Egypt. He proposed numerous other synchronisms stretching up to the time of Alexander the Great. He argued that these eliminate phantom dark ages and vindicate the Biblical accounts of history and those recorded by Herodotus.

Some of Velikovsky's specific hypothesized catastrophes included:

* A tentative suggestion that Earth had once been a satellite of a "proto-Saturn" body, before its current solar orbit.

* That the Deluge (Noah's Flood) had been caused by proto-Saturn entering a nova state, and ejecting much of its mass into space.

* A suggestion that the planet Mercury was involved in the Tower of Babel catastrophe.

* Jupiter had been the culprit for the catastrophe which saw the destruction of the "Cities of the Plain" (Sodom and Gomorrah)

* Periodic close contacts with a cometary Venus (which had been ejected from Jupiter) had caused the Exodus events (c.1500 B.C.E.) and Joshua's subsequent "sun standing still" incident.

* Periodic close contacts with Mars had caused havoc in the 8th and 7th centuries B.C.E.

Despite the attempts to silence his radical theories, Velikovsky's found enthusiastic, even exuberant supporters. The results were vehement public controversies that lasted for several decades. Velikovsky was interested in a serious, scientific discussion of his theories and made repeated efforts to initiate specific investigations, especially within the emerging space program. Unfortunately, he was met with scorn, ridicule, and even attempts at censorship, from the scientific community. His most vehement critics were often those who had not even read any of his books.

At the time, the notion proposed by Velikovsky that celestial bodies could somehow influence and cause destruction upon the Earth was considered scientific heresy. It is now accepted that a comet may have been responsible for wiping out the dinosaurs, yet in the 1950s, when Velikovsky suggested similar ideas, he was soundly rejected. Nevertheless the explorations of Venus, Mars and also of Saturn and Jupiter by space probes brought about findings, which Velikovsky, based on his studies, had already postulated years before. At the time he had earned fierce derision for it, and now these confirmations were mostly dismissed as chance hits. Even since the 1980s, when natural catastrophes became generally acknowledged as part of the history of the Earth, Velikovsky continues to be defamed or passed over in silence.

In fact many of his radical ideas that orthodox science originally laughed at, due to their lack of scientific foundation, have become proven facts:

* Jupiter periodically becomes unstable and ejects excess mass.

* Jupiter emits non-thermal radio noise.

* Comets can be rich in hydrocarbons, with highly energetic electrical tails.

* The Moon has had recent surface melting, seismic and volcanic activity, none of which should be true for a body that had supposedly been dead for 4.5 billion years.

Velikovsky deduced each of these facts many years before mainstream science found ways to prove them. He also stated that after its close encounters with Earth, Mars and the Sun, Venus would have a much higher than expected temperature, would be enveloped in hydrocarbon clouds (remnants of its comet's tail), and would have an anomalous rotation. The scientists' predictions – a similar temperature to Earth, an atmosphere of carbon dioxide or water and standard rotation – have all since been shown to be wrong. Venus has a surface temperature of 750 degrees Kelvin – hot enough to melt lead. Its atmosphere is full of hydrocarbons and its rotation is in an opposite direction to all the other planets.

Here is Velikovsky's hypothesis on what may have previously happened to our planet:

> ...that under the impact of a force or the influence of an agent – and the earth does not travel in an empty universe – the axis of the earth shifted or tilted. At that moment an earthquake would make the globe shudder. Air and water would continue to move through inertia; hurricanes would sweep the earth and the seas would rush over continents, carrying gravel and sand and marine animals, and casting them on the land. Heat would be developed, rocks would melt, volcanoes would erupt, and lava would flow from fissures in the ruptured ground and cover vast areas. Mountains would spring up from the plains and would travel and climb on the shoulders of other mountains, causing faults and rifts.

Lakes would be tilted and emptied, rivers would change their beds; large land areas with all their inhabitants would slip under the sea. Forests would burn, and the hurricanes and wild seas would wrest them from the ground on which they grew and pile them, branch and root, in huge heaps. Water evaporated from the oceans would rise in clouds and fall again in torrential rains and snowfalls. Clouds of dust ejected by numerous volcanoes and swept by hurricanes from the ground...all this dust would keep the rays of the sun from penetrating to the Earth.

Velikovsky stresses the information value of ancient texts, based according to him on real experiences lived in a different astronomical context than now. The idea that the events described in ancient texts pertained to real experiences used to be accepted without difficulty in western world until Illuminism. This included in particular the idea of catastrophes within human memory, including the Universal Deluge described in the Bible and in other traditions.

Illuminism started criticism of the Bible opening the way to the so-called uniformitarism approach that became dominant in the 19th century: the present is the key of the past, there are no celestial catastrophes today, and there were none in Moses time. No stones fall from the sky today, no stones could have fallen in the past (this extreme statement dominated astronomy well into the second half of 19th century, when a heavy fall of meteorites in France convinced the astronomers to accept ancient records of falling stones).

Now, fifty-eight years after *Worlds in Collision* we can certainly say that scholars in the natural sciences pay more attention to ancient records of catastrophes. Such attention is partly due also to the existence of technological means, not available at Velikovsky's time, to verify the effects of such unusual events in the geological and biological record. From such analysis evidence has emerged of strong climatic variations in the last 12,000 years, some setting so quickly that they can probably not be explained in terms of the usual terrestrial processes.

Finally, the direct observation in the case of the Shoemaker-Levy comet in the processes of disintegration and planetary impact, an event that astronomers considered extremely unlikely to be able to observe in their lifetime, has made the astronomical community conscious that our solar system is more fraught with dangers than it was believed just fifty years ago

Velikovsky has claimed the instability of the solar system and the emergence of the present orbital configuration, with regard at least to Mars and Venus, in very recent times, in fact in historical times (the last catastrophe, associated with Sennacherib siege of Jerusalem, being dated at about 27 centuries ago).

Such claims were made at a time when the solar system was considered to be an extremely stable configuration, on the basis of approximate analytical analysis of the stability of dynamical n-body systems and of the properties of the standard model (condensation from a gas cloud) for the formation of the solar system. This scenario after over fifty years has dramatically changed, albeit the thesis of Velikovsky about Venus and Mars is still considered unacceptable, except from a small minority of scholars.

The analysis made using modern analytical instruments has shown that the nonlinear, complex dynamical system, including planetary systems, can generally be defined as chaotic, whose long term behavior cannot be predicted and whose dynamical structure is extremely rich. Moreover, components of the solar system have been discovered, both at large distances or at planetary distances, that either were unknown 58 years ago, or their importance was not properly evaluated, e.g. the so called Apollo/Amor objects and the Kuiper belt (where objects of a considerable 600 km diameter are now known to exist).

The observation, albeit incomplete, of about sixty non solar planetary systems has shown dynamical and structural features completely unexpected and actually in several cases considered previously as dynamical impossibilities. For example the presence of Jovian or super Jovian planets very close to the mother star, when the current model had in that region only terrestrial type planets; or the presence of Jovian type planets in highly elliptical orbits.

Astronomer Tom Van Flandern has proposed the hypothesis originally suggested by Heinrich Wilhelm Matthäus Olbers about an explosion of one or more planets in the region of the asteroid belt. Van Flandern suggests that this event resulted in not only the asteroid belt, but also the majority of comets and possibly even Mars, considered as a surviving satellite of the exploded planet. Van Flandern dates the last explosion at 3.2 million years ago.

An independent observation by the physicists W. Woelfli and Walter Baltensperger finds that the sequence of ice ages on our planet also starts 3.2 million years ago. The physicists have proposed a new theory for the origin of such ice ages, in terms of effects on the Earth's axis, called true polar wandering (where the north and south points move over the Earth surface), due to the close flyby of a planet, whose size was almost identical to Mars.

Computer equations defining the dynamics of the flyby (considering only gravitational forces, but with heavy use of the tidal forces), show that a sufficiently close planetary passage can lead to a polar displacement of even 18 degrees, a conclusion that Velikovsky would have found to his liking. The two physicists also found that the planet interacting with Earth at its perihelion would be heated so much by the sun that it would move away looking like a giant comet, surrounded by bluish hot gas over one million miles in diameter.

Even though Velikovsky is still considered a pariah within scientific circles, the theory of catastrophism has returned thanks to new scientific research and a better understanding of the cosmos. One impetus for this change came from the publication of a historic paper by Walter and Luis Alvarez in 1980. This paper suggested that an 11-mile wide asteroid struck the Earth 65 million years ago at the end of the Cretaceous period. The impact wiped out about 70% of all species, including the dinosaurs, leaving behind the so-called K-T boundary. In 1990, a 180-mile wide crater marking the impact was identified at Chicxulub in the Yucatán Peninsula of Mexico.

Since then, the debate about the extinction of the dinosaurs and other mass extinction events has centered on whether the extinction mechanism was the asteroid impact, widespread volcanism (which occurred about the same time), or some other mechanism or combination. Most of the mechanisms suggested are catastrophic in nature.

Modern theories also suggest that Earth's anomalously large moon was formed catastrophically. In a paper published in Icarus in 1975, Dr. William K. Hartmann and Dr. Donald R. Davis proposed that a stochastic catastrophic near-miss by a large planetesimal early in Earth's formation approximately 4.5 billion years ago blew out rocky debris, re-melted Earth and formed the Moon, thus explaining the Moon's lesser density and lack of an iron core.

Today most geologists accept the catastrophic theory, taking the view that Earth's history is a slow, gradual story punctuated by occasional natural catastrophic events that have affected Earth and its inhabitants.

Even though no one is willing to admit that a Russian psychiatrist, using ancient myths and folktales, may have discovered that the Earth has suffered catastrophic close-encounters with other planets, perhaps it is time for academia to put aside their prejudice and re-examine the works of Immanuel Velikovsky. There is no telling what new scientific discoveries and startling ideas await within the books of one of the most original and controversial thinkers of the 20th century.

CHAPTER SIX
Prophets and Prophecies

In examining the theories of Zechariah Sitchin, Immanuel Velikovsky, and others, we are left with the conclusion that it is entirely possible that in the past, planet Earth has suffered massive destruction and catastrophic changes due to interactions with other celestial bodies. Even though there is considerable testimony that Planet X, or Nibiru may reenter the solar system sometime after 2012, Zechariah Sitchin dismisses these theories and says that there is no evidence that Nibiru is going to make an appearance anytime soon.

So what do the prophets have to say about the return of Planet X? If such a physical and spiritual event is actually going to happen, there should be sufficient psychic energies resonating from that date and into the past for any self-respecting prophet to pick up on.

The Maya, as a people were not prophets, this is not to say that there weren't individual prophets, but certainly their major system of plotting future events was not reliant upon prophets. The Maya did have great interest in esoteric matters; they had a pantheon of gods and at times accredited supernatural powers to certain persons as well as to animals and objects. The trouble is that modern writers are sometimes too quick in amalgamating these two distinct aspects of ancient Mayan society and allowing the mix to color the scientific basis for concern regarding the calendar end date.

It is essential to show that in the end, the Mayan calendar is not giving us a doomsday prophecy comparable to those of the now legendary French prophet Michel De Nostradame. This is something that is essentially a modern concept that has used the Mayan calendar to enforce a Judeo-Christian belief structure. This notion views as inevitable that there will be an "end" to the current sinful times and the beginning of the reign of God on Earth. However, there are other prophecies from various sources around the world that have come out to state expectations regarding the end of the world due to their own mystical ideas and traditions.

Every generation thinks that they just may be the last generation to walk the planet. People seem to have an almost perverse pleasure in frightening themselves into believing that the "end of days" is close at hand. Many hope for the end of the world because it fulfills a desire to see divine punishment for those who are considered sinners, unbelievers, or unworthy. Others hope for the return of deities and the resurrection of long passed loved ones. And there are those who simply cannot conceive the world continuing to exist past their own short life span.

Despite the predictions, despite the prophecies, despite the worry, the world continues to spin in its orbit and life goes on. But people cannot help but to look apprehensively towards the future. Surely something will happen someday...someone pushes the wrong button, sending nuclear-tipped missiles flying...a plague will strike...a comet will hit...a nearby star will go supernova. There are just so many things that can go wrong that statistically, the chances are pretty good that something bad will occur someday.

When the end of the world does come about, and everything is left a smoking ruin; it is almost a certainty that there will be someone left to shout to the smoldering ashes, "I Told You So!"

MOTHER SHIPTON'S PROPHECIES

Mother Shipton was born Ursula Sontheil in 1488 in Knaresborough near Harrogate North Yorkshire, England, and died in 1561. Her mother, Agatha, was reputed to be a witch, and Mother Shipton is said to have exhibited prophetic and psychic abilities from an early age. At 24, she married Toby Shipton and eventually became known as Mother Shipton (some times also known as 'Old Mother Shipton').

An 18th century biographer described Mother Shipton's appearance in these words: "Her stature was larger than common, her body crooked, her face frightful, but her understanding extraordinary."

An ancient Scottish chronicle reports that her entrance into the world was attended by "various wonderful presages."

"A raven croaked upon the chimney top; an extraordinary noise was heard about the house for several nights before; and a violent storm of thunder and rain was the immediate precursor of her arrival. It was also observed that as soon as she was born, she fell a grinning and laughing, after a jeering manner, and immediately the tempest ceased."

Mother Shipton was a seeress who lived in England. Born in 1488, she poured her prophetic visions into poetry. One of the most intriguing parts of her prophecies covers a celestial event of tremendous proportions that may point to the return of Planet X

Out Of The Darkness – UFO Revelations And Planet X

Even as a young woman, Ursula had already begun to gain something of a reputation as a soothsayer. This reputation extended beyond her local area – people traveled to Knaresborough from some distance around to consult her. Although her appearance, recorded as "a body larger than common, and crooked with a face frightful to look upon," well suited her to play the role of the witch of contemporary popular imaginings, she is also described as "extraordinary" in her compassion and understanding.

Mother Shipton seems to have been particularly successful in solving the sort of interpersonal disputes that must have been as commonplace then as now and few appeals for help from wronged townsfolk went unresolved. This pattern seems to have been established very early in her married life and continued until her death. Thieves would publicly return stolen goods, apologizing to the astonished owners for their sin; wandering husbands would beg forgiveness and mend their ways; corrupt officials would make spontaneous acts of restitution.

It is easy to see how she might have used an insider's knowledge of her neighbors – and perhaps a measure of coercion – to bring about these results and perhaps even apparently to "predict" the future within the confines of her own small community. For an astute woman, as she undoubtedly was, the signs of blooming love, illness and death are always there to be read. However, some of her prophesies cannot be explained away so readily, although her habit of making them in riddles, as her close contemporary Nostradamus had done, does rather leave some of them open to a fair degree of "interpretation" after the fact.

Nevertheless, Mother Shipton's words are said to have foretold much of the future history of England, including Drake's defeat of the Spanish Armada, the execution of Mary, Queen of Scots, and the succession of James VI of Scotland (and I of England) and union between the two countries. Over 105 years after her death, as the Great Fire of London began just a year after the ravages of the Great Plague, the famous diarist Samuel Pepys wrote "See – Mother Shipton's word is out." It also said that she predicted the time of her own death, supposedly to the very day and hour.

Mother Shipton is credited with predicting many aspects of everyday life that would have seemed outrageous and inconceivable in her time – automobiles and trains, iron ships, submarines, aircraft, telegraphy, and possibly by extension, even the Internet. However, it is now widely thought that many of these apparently prophetic writings have been added to her list years after her death.

As for her prophecies, the earliest pamphlets and books about Mother Shipton were published in 1641 and 1684. We may never

Out Of The Darkness – UFO Revelations And Planet X

know for sure if a person named Mother Shipton actually existed. We are, however, left with a puzzling series of prophecies that even if they were not originally written by the witch of Knaresborough, nevertheless show a great insight for future days and possible "events in the heavens" around the year 2012.

>And now a word, in uncouth rhyme
>Of what shall be in future time.
>
>Then upside down the world shall be
>And gold found at the root of tree
>All England's sons that plough the land
>Shall oft be seen with Book in hand.
>
>The poor shall now great wisdom know
>Great houses stand in far-flung vale
>All covered o'er with snow and hail.
>A carriage without horse will go
>Disaster fill the world with woe.
>
>In London, Primrose Hill shall be
>In centre hold a Bishop's See
>Around the world men's thoughts will fly
>Quick as the twinkling of an eye.
>
>And water shall great wonders do
>How strange. And yet it shall come true.
>Through towering hills proud men shall ride
>No horse or ass move by his side.
>
>Beneath the water, men shall walk
>Shall ride, shall sleep, shall even talk.
>And in the air men shall be seen
>In white and black and even green.
>
>A great man then, shall come and go
>For prophecy declares it so.
>In water, iron, then shall float
>As easy as a wooden boat
>Gold shall be seen in stream and stone
>In land that is yet unknown.
>
>And England shall admit a Jew
>You think this strange, but it is true
>The Jew that once was held in scorn

Out Of The Darkness – UFO Revelations And Planet X

Shall of a Christian then be born.

A house of glass shall come to pass
In England. But Alas, alas
A war will follow with the work
Where dwells the Pagan and the Turk.

These states will lock in fiercest strife
And seek to take each other's life.
When North shall thus divide the south
And Eagle build in Lion's mouth
Then tax and blood and cruel war
Shall come to every humble door.

Three times shall lovely sunny France
Be led to play a bloody dance
Before the people shall be free
Three tyrant rulers shall she see.

Three rulers in succession be
Each springs from different dynasty.
Then when the fiercest strife is done
England and France shall be as one.
The British olive shall next then twine
In marriage with a German vine.
Men walk beneath and over streams
Fulfilled shall be their wondrous dreams.

For in those wondrous far off days
The women shall adopt a craze
To dress like men, and trousers wear
And to cut off their locks of hair.
They'll ride astride with brazen brow
As witches do on broomstick now.

And roaring monsters with man atop
Does seem to eat the verdant crop
And men shall fly as birds do now
And give away the horse and plough.

There'll be a sign for all to see
Be sure that it will certain be.
Then love shall die and marriage cease
And nations wane as babes decrease.
And wives shall fondle cats and dogs

Out Of The Darkness – UFO Revelations And Planet X

And men live much the same as hogs.

In nineteen hundred and twenty six
Build houses light of straw and sticks.
For then shall mighty wars be planned
And fire and sword shall sweep the land.

When pictures seem alive with movements free
When boats like fishes swim beneath the sea,
When men like birds shall scour the sky
Then half the world, deep drenched in blood shall die.

For those who live the century through
In fear and trembling this shall do.
Flee to the mountains and the dens
To bog and forest and wild fens.
For storms will rage and oceans roar
When Gabriel stands on sea and shore
And as he blows his wondrous horn
Old worlds die and new be born.
A fiery Dragon will cross the sky
Six times before this earth shall die
Mankind will tremble and frightened be
For the sixth heralds in this prophecy.

For seven days and seven nights
Man will watch this awesome sight.
The tides will rise beyond their ken
To bite away the shores and then
The mountains will begin to roar
And earthquakes split the plain to shore.

And flooding waters, rushing in
Will flood the lands with such a din
That mankind cowers in muddy fen
And snarls about his fellow men.

He bares his teeth and fights and kills
And secrets food in secret hills
And ugly in his fear, he lies
To kill marauders, thieves and spies.

Man flees in terror from the floods
And kills, and rapes and lies in blood
And spilling blood by mankind's hands

Out Of The Darkness – UFO Revelations And Planet X

Will stain and bitter many lands.

And when the Dragon's tail is gone,
Man forgets, and smiles, and carries on
To apply himself – too late, too late
For mankind has earned deserved fate.

His masked smile – his false grandeur
Will serve the Gods their anger stir.
And they will send the Dragon back
To light the sky – his tail will crack
Upon the earth and rend the earth
And man shall flee, King, Lord, and serf.

But slowly they are routed out
To seek diminishing water spout
And men will die of thirst before
The oceans rise to mount the shore.
And lands will crack and rend anew
You think it strange. It will come true.

And in some far off distant land
Some men – oh such a tiny band
Will have to leave their solid mount
And span the earth, those few to count,
Who survives this (unreadable) and then
Begin the human race again.

But not on land already there
But on ocean beds, stark, dry and bare
Not every soul on Earth will die
As the Dragon's tail goes sweeping by.

Not every land on earth will sink
But these will wallow in stench and stink
Of rotting bodies of beast and man
Of vegetation crisped on land.

But the land that rises from the sea
Will be dry and clean and soft and free
Of mankind's dirt and therefore be
The source of man's new dynasty.

And those that live will ever fear
The Dragons tail for many year

Out Of The Darkness – UFO Revelations And Planet X

But time erases memory
You think it strange. But it will be.

And before the race is built anew
A silver serpent comes to view
And spew out men of like unknown
To mingle with the earth now grown
Cold from its heat and these men can
Enlighten the minds of future man.
To intermingle and show them how
To live and love and thus endow
The children with the second sight.
A natural thing so that they might
Grow graceful, humble and when they do
The Golden Age will start anew.

I know I go – I know I'm free
I know that this will come to be.
Secreted this – for this will be
Found by later dynasty.

A dairy maid, a bonny lass
Shall kick this tome as she does pass
And five generations she shall breed
Before one male child does learn to read.

This is then held year by year
Till an iron monster trembling fear
Eats parchment, words and quill and ink
And mankind is given time to think.

And only when this comes to be
Will mankind read this prophecy
But one man's sweet's another's bane
So I shall not have burned in vain.

The signs will be there for all to read
When man shall do most heinous deed
Man will ruin kinder lives
By taking them as to their wives.
And murder foul and brutal deed
When man will only think of greed.

And man shall walk as if asleep
He does not look – he many not peep

And iron men the tail shall do
And iron cart and carriage too.
The kings shall false promise make
And talk just for talking's sake
And nations plan horrific war
The like as never seen before.
And taxes rise and lively down
And nations wear perpetual frown.

Yet greater sign there be to see
As man nears latter century.
Three sleeping mountains gather breath
And spew out mud, and ice and death.
And earthquakes swallow town and town,
In lands as yet to me unknown.

And Christian one fights Christian two
And nations sigh, yet nothing do
And yellow men great power gain
From mighty bear with whom they've lain.

These mighty tyrants will fail to do
They fail to split the world in two.
But from their acts a danger bred
An ague – leaving many dead.

And physics find no remedy
For this is worse than leprosy.
Oh many signs for all to see
The truth of this true prophecy.

Mother Shipton

THE PROPHECY OF PETER DEUNOV

Known under the spiritual name of Beinsa Douno, the Bulgarian Master, Peter Deunov (1864-1944) was the son of an orthodox pope and destined to become a member of the clergy. He studied theology followed by medicine in the United States, but after his return to Bulgaria in 1895, he did not fit well in the rigid context of the institutions and dogmas of the orthodox Church.

From 1900, he began to give public lectures that breathed a new life to the traditional Christian doctrines. Deunov reportedly had a very high level of consciousness and demonstrated during his entire life an example of purity, wisdom, intelligence and creativity. As well, he was an accomplished violinist who created hundreds of melodies and songs that became spiritual exercises in the school, The White Brotherhood, he founded at the turn of the 20th century.

For years he was established close to the capital city of Sofia where he lived surrounded by numerous disciples. It is said that Deunov awakened the spirituality of thousands of souls in Bulgaria as well as the rest of Europe. The philosopher René Guenon lauded Deunov in this way: "He is the greatest spiritual magnet yet able to appear on the earth. He will magnetize his disciples with the magnetism of love, and they in turn will transmit this magnetism to humankind as a whole."

In the days before his death, Deunov was in a profound mediumistic trance. While in this trance, he made an extraordinary prophecy in regards to our troubled times – a prophecy about the "end of time" and the coming of a new Golden Age of humanity.

> During the passage of time, the consciousness of man traversed a very long period of obscurity. This phase which the Hindus call "Kali Yuga," is on the verge of ending. We find ourselves today at the frontier between two epochs: that of Kali Yuga and that of the New Era that we are entering.
>
> A gradual improvement is already occurring in the thoughts, sentiments and acts of humans, but everybody will soon be subjugated to divine Fire, that will purify and prepare them in regards to the New Era. Thus man will raise himself to a superior degree of consciousness, indispensable to his entrance to the New Life. That is what one understands by "Ascension."
>
> Some decades will pass before this Fire will come, that will transform the world by bringing it a new moral. This immense wave comes from cosmic space and will inundate the entire earth. All those that attempt to oppose it will be carried off and transferred elsewhere.
>
> Although the inhabitants of this planet do not all find themselves at the same degree of evolution, the new wave will be felt by each one of us. And this transformation will not only touch the Earth, but the ensemble of the entire Cosmos.
>
> The best and only thing that man can do now is to turn towards God and improve himself consciously, to elevate his vibratory level, so as to find himself in harmony with the powerful wave that will soon submerge him.

Out Of The Darkness – UFO Revelations And Planet X

The Fire of which I speak, that accompanies the new conditions offered to our planet, will rejuvenate, purify, reconstruct everything: the matter will be refined, your hearts will be liberated from anguish, troubles, incertitude, and they will become luminous; everything will be improved, elevated; the thoughts, sentiments and negative acts will be consumed and destroyed.

Your present life is slavery, a heavy prison. Understand your situation and liberate yourself from it. I tell you this: exit from your prison! It is really sorry to see so much misleading, so much suffering, so much incapacity to understand where one's true happiness lies.

Everything that is around you will soon collapse and disappear. Nothing will be left of this civilization nor its perversity; the entire earth will be shaken and no trace will be left of this erroneous culture that maintains men under the yoke of ignorance. Earthquakes are not only mechanical phenomenon, their goal is also to awaken the intellect and the heart of humans, so that they liberate themselves from their errors and their follies and that they understand that they are not the only ones in the universe.

Our solar system is now traversing a region of the Cosmos where a constellation that was destroyed left its mark, its dust. This crossing of a contaminated space is a source of poisoning, not only for the inhabitants of the Earth, but for all the inhabitants of the other planets of our galaxy. Only the suns are not affected by the influence of this hostile environment. This region is called "the thirteenth zone," one also calls it "the zone of contradictions." Our planet was enclosed in this region for thousands of years, but finally we are approaching the exit of this space of darkness and we are on the point of attaining a more spiritual region, where more evolved beings live.

The Earth is now following an ascending movement and everyone should force themselves to harmonize with the currents of the ascension. Those who refuse to subjugate themselves to this orientation will lose the advantage of good conditions that are offered in the future to elevate themselves. They will remain behind in evolution and must wait tens of millions of years for the coming of a new ascending wave.

Out Of The Darkness – UFO Revelations And Planet X

The Earth, the solar system, the universe, all are being put in a new direction under the impulsion of Love. Most of you still consider Love as a derisory force, but in reality, it is the greatest of all forces! Money and power continue to be venerated as if the course of your life depended upon it. In the future, all will be subjugated to Love and all will serve it. But it is through suffering and difficulties that the consciousness of man will be awakened.

The terrible predictions of the prophet Daniel written in the bible relate to the epoch that is opening. There will be floods, hurricanes, gigantic fires and earthquakes that will sweep away everything. Blood will flow in abundance. There will be revolutions; terrible explosions will resound in numerous regions of the earth. There where there is earth, water will come, and there where there is water, earth will come. God is Love; yet we are dealing here with a chastisement, a reply by Nature against the crimes perpetrated by man since the night of time against his Mother; the Earth.

After these sufferings, those that will be saved, the elite, will know the Golden Age, harmony and unlimited beauty. Thus keep your peace and your faith when the time comes for suffering and terror, because it is written that not a hair will fall from the head of the just. Don't be discouraged; simply follow your work of personal perfection.

You have no idea of the grandiose future that awaits you. A New Earth will soon see day. In a few decades the work will be less exacting, and each one will have the time to consecrate spiritual, intellectual and artistic activities. The question of rapport between man and woman will be finally resolved in harmony; each one having the possibility of following their aspirations. The relations of couples will be founded on reciprocal respect and esteem. Humans will voyage through the different planes of space and breakthrough intergalactic space. They will study their functioning and will rapidly be able to know the Divine World, to fusion with the Head of the Universe.

The New Era is that of the sixth race. Your predestination is to prepare yourself for it, to welcome it and to live it. The sixth race will build itself around the idea of Fraternity. There will be no more conflicts of personal interests; the single aspiration of each one will be to conform himself to the Law of Love. The sixth race will be that of Love. A new continent will be formed for it. It will emerge from the Pacific, so that the Most High can finally establish His place on this planet.

The founders of this new civilization, I call them "Brothers of Humanity" or also "Children of Love." They will be unshakeable for the good and they will represent a new type of men. Men will form a family, as a large body, and each people will represent an organ in this body. In the new race, Love will manifest in such a perfect manner, that today's man can only have a very vague idea.

The Earth will remain a terrain favorable to struggle, but the forces of darkness will retreat and the earth will be liberated from them. Humans seeing that there is no other path will engage themselves to the path of the New Life, that of salvation. In their senseless pride, some will, to the end hope to continue on earth a life that the Divine Order condemns, but each one will finish by understanding that the direction of the world doesn't belong to them.

A new culture will see the light of day; it will rest on three principal foundations: the elevation of woman, the elevation of the meek and humble, and the protection of the rights of man.

The light, the good, and justice will triumph; it is just a question of time. The religions should be purified. Each contains a particle of the Teaching of the Masters of Light, but obscured by the incessant supply of human deviation. All the believers will have to unite and to put themselves in agreement with one principal that of placing Love as the base of all belief, whatever it may be. Love and Fraternity that is the common base!

The Earth will soon be swept by extraordinary rapid waves of Cosmic Electricity. A few decades from now beings that are bad and lead others astray will not be able to support their intensity. They will thus be absorbed by Cosmic Fire that will consume the bad that they possess. Then they will repent because it is written that "each flesh shall glorify God."

Our mother, the Earth, will get rid of men that don't accept the New Life. She will reject them like damaged fruit. They will soon not be able to reincarnate on this planet; criminals included. Only those that possess Love in them will remain.

There is not any place on Earth that is not dirtied with human or animal blood; she must therefore submit to purification. And it is for this that certain continents will be immersed while others will surface.

Men do not suspect to what dangers they are menaced by. They continue to pursue futile objectives and to seek pleasure. On the contrary those of the sixth race will be conscious of the dignity of their role and respectful of each one's liberty. They will nourish themselves exclusively from products of the vegetal realm. Their ideas will have the power to circulate freely as the air and light of our days.

The words "If you are not born again." apply to the sixth race. Read Chapter 60 of Isaiah it relates to the coming of the sixth race the Race of Love.

After the Tribulations, men will cease to sin and will find again the path of virtue. The climate of our planet will be moderated everywhere and brutal variations will no longer exist. The air will once again become pure, the same for water. The parasites will disappear. Men will remember their previous incarnations and they will feel the pleasure of noticing that they are finally liberated from their previous condition.

In the same manner that one gets rid of the parasites and dead leaves on the vine, so act the evolved Beings to prepare men to serve the God of Love. They give to them good conditions to grow and to develop themselves, and to those that want to listen to them, they say: "Do not be afraid! Still a little more time and everything will be all right; you are on the good path. May he that wants to enter in the New Culture study, consciously work and prepare."

Thanks to the idea of Fraternity, the Earth will become a blessed place, and that will not wait. But before, great sufferings will be sent to awaken the consciousness. Sins accumulated for thousands of years must be redeemed. The ardent wave emanating from On High will contribute in liquidating the karma of peoples.

The liberation can no longer be postponed. Humanity must prepare itself for great trials that are inescapable and are coming to bring an end to egoism.

Under the Earth, something extraordinary is preparing itself. A revolution that is grandiose and completely inconceivable will manifest itself soon in nature. God has decided to redress the Earth and He will do it!

It is the end of an epoch; a new order will substitute the old, an order in which Love will reign on Earth."

Peter Deunov – Prophecies on the Future – 1944
Adaptation: Olivier de Rouvroy - September 2003

PROPHECIES OF THE KING OF AGHARTI

For many centuries, the mysterious and mystical tradition of Agharti and its ruler, the King of the World, has existed in Tibet and Mongolia. Agharti is believed by many to be a real world existing under the high plateau in the mountains of Central Asia. It is said to be a series of huge caverns with secret entrances all over the Earth. Ancient tribes sometimes entered and have maintained a hidden civilization to this very day.

This underground version of Shangri-la still exists, according to belief, and, whenever the King of the World makes prophecies, the birds and animals on the surface suddenly become silent. Hundreds of years ago, the King of the World uttered a prophecy which, counting from the time it was purportedly given, falls, as do so many other predictions, within the latter part of the 20th Century.

> Men will increasingly neglect their souls. The greatest corruption will reign on earth. Men will become like bloodthirsty animals, thirsting for the blood of their brothers. The crescent will become obscured, and its followers will descend into lies and perpetual warfare. The crowns of kings will fall.
> There will be terrible war between all the earth's peoples; entire nations will die – hunger, crimes unknown to law, formerly unthinkable to the world. The persecuted will demand the attention of the whole world. The ancient roads will be filled with multitudes going from one place to another. The greatest and most beautiful cities will perish by fire. Families will be dispersed; faith and love will disappear. The world will be emptied.
> Within fifty years there will be only three great nations. Then, within fifty years, there will be 18 years of war and cataclysms. Then the peoples of Agharti will

leave their subterranean caverns and will appear on the surface of the Earth.

RUTH MONTGOMERY

Ruth Montgomery (1913 - 2001), a past president of the prestigious National Press Club, began her career as a Washington DC reporter. She wrote a book about the world-renowned psychic, Jeanne Dixon, called *A Gift of Prophecy*. Jeanne Dixon was the psychic who warned President Kennedy not to go to Dallas on that fateful day. Her book on Dixon was very successful and Montgomery began looking further into the paranormal phenomenon. She soon discovered that she had the gift of "automatic writing" by which she could communicate with various deceased personalities.

Despite all the ridicule and criticism, she was able to channel a great deal of information from the other side, specifically from her deceased friend, the famous spiritualist and medium, Arthur Ford. In her book, *Strangers Among Us*, written in 1979, Montgomery is told by her spirit guides to look for an absolutely unavoidable shift in the Earth's axis and crust sometime in the early 21st century.

The shift will have its warnings. The revolutions of the Earth will start to slow down. The weather will be worsening in most areas, with storms becoming increasingly violent, with heavy snowfalls, strong gales, and increased humidity. There will be rumblings beneath the Earth, and the trees will sway. Shortly before the actual shift, there will be two specific types of warnings. The eruptions of ancient volcanoes in Mediterranean islands, South America and California will result in pestilence, and shortly there after earth tremors of major proportions, affecting wide land-masses in northern Europe, Asia, and South America, will provoke tidal waves of incredible scale.

For days and nights before the shift, the earth will seem to rock gently. The spirit guides said some will recognize this as the time to remove themselves quickly from the seacoasts and other exposed places, and while that exodus is occurring there will be increasing earthquakes, and volcanic eruptions in flat areas that had previously shown no sign of such disturbances. Some will remain despite the alarms, disbelieving that a shift will occur; and some, deciding that it is a good time to return to spirit, will refuse to leave their homes.

The Earth will hesitate in its orbit prior to the shift. In daylight areas, the sun will seem to stand still overhead, and then to race backward for the brief period while the Earth settles into its new position relative to the sun. In nighttime areas, the stars will seem to swing giddily in the heavens, and as dawn breaks the sun will seemingly rise from the wrong place on the horizon. Those who are capable of reaching safety will see the Earth's surface tremble, shudder, and in some places become a sea of boiling water.

Simultaneous explosions beneath the planet's crust will bring new land above the surface of the waters, as other areas are swallowed by the sea. For the survivors there will be anguish and heartache, but also exhilaration in having withstood the ferocity of nature and most of those remaining will feel that God saved them for a purpose.

There will be dramatic climate changes. Some cold places will become warm and some warm places will freeze over. Countless numbers of humans, animals, and birds will freeze to death where the new poles settle.

Ferocious and devastatingly high winds will sweep away most above ground structures. New York City will vanish. Florida will scarcely survive, except as scattered islands. The southern states bordering the Atlantic and Gulf of Mexico will be drastically altered, including parts of Texas. In the west, the remainder of California will disappear beneath the broiling waves. Canada will be in warmer latitudes and much of it will be relatively safe from sinking or destruction by tidal waves. Washington DC will be devastated, but not totally destroyed being near the mountains. Government workers will carry on in the previously prepared shelters hidden away beneath the ground.

MAYAN PROPHESIES FOR THE NEW MILLENNIUM

The Mayan prophecies are being fulfilled. Some are being fulfilled even now. Some will be fulfilled on the morrow. The Mayan prophecies exist because the Mayas knew the cosmic time. They knew that in certain times it would be necessary to keep this cosmic wisdom secret. This was the purpose of the prophecy so that they might be able to communicate their secrets to the initiates of the future.

It is prophesied that initiates shall return to the sacred land of the Mayas to continue the work of the Great Spirit. Here in the lands of the Mayab, in the cycle of light, there surged a great wisdom, which would illuminate humanity for many millennia. This wisdom was given to the Mayan-Itzaes.

Now the reincarnated masters return to these lands of the Mayan to communicate with the great spirits of the Itzaes so that together they may understand what shall be the new initiation which will be put to practice; so that humanity, the reincarnated masters and the great spirits of the Itzaes may fuse into one. Then they will be able to travel like the wind, descend like the rain, give warmth like fire and teach like Mother Earth.

These masters will come from many places. They will be of many colors. Some will speak of things difficult to understand. Others will be aged; some less so. Some will dance while others will remain silent as rocks. Their eyes will communicate the initiatic message, which is to continue through the cycles of the next millennium.

It is also prophesied that this initiation of cosmic wisdom is for future initiates. They will be young and old, men and women who will have the understanding that this modern civilization is not meeting its educational responsibilities. It is well known that this so-called modern civilization has caused a regressive effect in spiritual development.

The Mayan ceremonial centers begin to emanate the light of the new millennium, which is much needed today. Many Mayan cosmic ceremonial centers begin to beckon, with their solar reflection, the many initiates who will come to continue the work of the Great Spirit. In many Mayan ceremonial centers Solar Priests will begin to walk among the multitude of tourists. They will be touched by the Solar Priests to be initiation with the cosmic wisdom. It will be then that the initiates of the second level shall begin to work among the new initiates."

Elder Hunbatz Men

ANCIENT PROPHECIES FOR MODERN TIMES

Hunbatz Men tells of an ancient confederation of Native American elders made up of representatives from Nicaragua to the Arctic Circle. They have been meeting for thousands of years and continue to do so today. Before the Spaniards came the confederation decided to hide the Mayan teachings, entrusting certain families with their care. Hunbatz Men is an inheritor of that lineage. In his book Secrets of Mayan Science/ Religion, he reveals teachings that mirror the Hindu and Buddhist ones of astrology, meditation, and the septenary root of creation.

He speaks of Kukulcan and Quetzalcoatl, not so much in light of an expected return, but rather in terms of the possibility that each of us can attain the same exalted stage by treading the path of attaining knowledge. "To be Quetzalcoatl or Kukulcan is to know the seven forces that govern our body - not only know them but also use them and understand their intimate relationship with natural and cosmic laws. We must comprehend the long and short cycles and the solar laws that sustain our lives. We must know how to die, and how to be born."

Don Alejandro Oxlaj is a seventh generation priest from Guatemala and head of the Quiche Maya Elder Council. He has traveled throughout North America, comparing the native prophecies of different tribes. In the coming year he hopes to record and publish, for the first time in 500 years, the Mayan prophecies of his people.

What is enlightening in all of these statements is their consistent tone of reconciliation. The native groups are opening their doors to people of every color, speaking of themselves as Rainbow Warriors. Their elders have reminded them to "remember the original instructions" when each tribe was given by the creator a mandate to follow. That mandate has told them that now is the time to heal the past, despite the centuries of pain and persecution. Now is the time to join together and work in harmony to rehabilitate the planet and establish an era of alignment and peace."

Bette Stockbauer

MAYAN PROPHECY: THE REAWAKENING OF THE COSMIC MAN

In 1475, seventeen years before Christopher Columbus made his first journey to the "New World," the Supreme Maya Priestly Council assembled to reveal that darkness would soon be failing upon the Mayan people and that two calendar cycles would have to pass before the Mayan people would once again emerge into the light. Considering the devastation suffered by the Maya at the hands of the Spanish Conquistadors, the prediction of darkness was amazingly accurate.

According to Mayan calendar keeper, Hunbatz Men, the Spring Equinox (March 21) of 1995 marked the end of that period of darkness; since 520 years have now passed (each Mayan calendar cycle is 260 years). To mark the event, Hunbatz Men led a solar initiation on this date at Chichen Itz, one of the largest and most frequently visited ruins in the Yucatan Peninsula.

This initiation offered a genuine spiritual experience for the tens of thousands who attended, most of whom were Mayan. The day was filled with wonder: Lamas from Tibet and leaders of the Supreme Mayan Council bestowed blessings upon attendees; Mayan music and dance was performed on stage; and the incredible architecture of Chichen Itz was available for all to view.

The ceremony came to a climax late in the afternoon when a shadow image of the serpent appeared on the Pyramid of Kukulcan. This image appears bi-annually at Chichen Itz and is a testament to the architectural and astronomical talents of Mayan civilization. At the Equinox, the sun hits in such a way that a shadow forms on one of the pyramid's edges in the shape of a serpent's body. This shadow snake connects with a statue of a serpent's head at base of the pyramid to complete the image of a holy Mayan symbol, representing fertility and re-birth. Attendees responded with meditation, chanting, and prayer, and displayed reverence for the miracle.

As we reflect on the event, it is hard not to think about the recent birth of a white buffalo in Janesville, Wisconsin. This unique appearance fulfills an ancient Indian prophecy and signifies a new period of hope and renewal for Native American culture. According to the Lakota Sioux, the birth of a female white buffalo promises unity among people and a new respect for the earth. Let's hope both of these prophecies may be fulfilled.

Aluna Joy Yaxk'in

DOOMSDAY, THEN AND NOW

In TIMAEUS, written about 400 BCE, or approximately 300 years following the final departure of the Planet Nibiru in 687 B.C.E., Plato recorded a journey to Egypt by Solon, a Greek philosopher. The Egyptian priests related to Solon the story of Atlantis and its destruction. In connection with this story, an Egyptian priest had the following to say:

"There have been, and there will be again, many destructions of Mankind arising out of many causes. There is a story which even you Greeks have preserved that once upon a time, Phaëthon, the son of Helios, having yoked the steeds of his father's chariot, because he was not able to drive them in the path of his father, burnt up all that was upon the Earth, and was himself destroyed by a thunderbolt. Now this has the form of a myth, but really signifies a deviation from their courses of the bodies moving around the Earth and in the Heavens, and a great conflagration of things upon the Earth recurring at long intervals of time. When this conflagration happens, those who live upon the mountains and in dry and lofty places are more liable to destruction than those who dwell by rivers or on the seashore; and from this calamity the fact that we live on the low-lying land by the Nile, who is our never-failing savior, saves and delivers us.

"When, on the other hand, the Gods purge the Earth with a deluge of water, amongst you herdsmen and shepherds on the mountains are the survivors, whereas those of you who live in cities are swept by the waters into the sea; but in this country neither at that time nor at any other does the water come from above on the fields, having always a tendency to come up from below, for which reason the things preserved here are said to be the oldest.

"The fact is that, wherever the extremity of winter frost or of summer sun does not prevent, the human race is always increasing at times, and at other times diminishing in numbers. As for those genealogies of yours which you have recounted to us, Solon, they are no better than the tales of children; for, in the first place, you remember one deluge only, whereas there were many before that; and, in the next place, you do not know that there dwelt in your land the fairest and noblest race of men which ever lived, of whom you and your whole city of Athens are but a seed or remnant. And this was unknown to you, because for many generations the survivors of that destruction died and made no sign.

"There was a time, Solon, before that great deluge of all, when the city which is now Athens was first in war, and pre-eminent for the excellence of her laws, and is said to have performed the noblest deeds, and to have had the fairest constitution of any of which tradition tells, under the face of Heaven."

As we move deeper and deeper into the Nibiru's comet-like tail the situation will deteriorate rapidly. What used to be merely an "annoying red dust" will become larger and ever larger in size, from dust to gravel to rocks to boulders. Eventually, it will become a "rain of stones" varying in size from snowflakes to beachballs. "All the mansions of Earth will fall." At this point, whether one has a home-insurance policy from the Hartford will not matter. We shall be on our own.

As the Papyrus Ipuwer informs us, those who remained indoors were crushed to death when their houses were smashed by falling boulders. Those who ventured outdoors to escape being killed in their houses were stoned to death in the streets. Damage would undoubtedly resemble what happens when a killer tornado rips through a neighborhood. We can only huddle in the sturdiest parts of our houses and pray that we will survive. But many of these falling stones will be flaming meteorites which, in turn, will ignite massive fires in urban and rural areas, home fires as well as forest fires. By this point in time, without a doubt, all electric power and running water will cease. Fearful thundering noises will echo throughout the heavens.

As the rain of stones begins to subside, electrical sparks will jump and hiss between these two "clashing worlds." Depending upon the electromagnetic intensity of these sparks, which are prelude to the establishment of the tethering beam, the "tree trunk," any data stored on Earth by magnetic methods, including computer data, CDs, tape recordings (audio or video) and such like, will be damaged or completely erased. This will be the most devastating consequence of the encounter, because it has the potential to destroy the Internet along with telephone and other communications technologies. Those who still survive will not only be hungry and thirsty, probably injured by falling rocks, but in all likelihood will be totally out of communication with everyone except those in their immediate neighborhoods.

Needless to say, by this point in time, those who are still alive will be in a state of shock, which is an understatement. And there's one thing that we can predict with absolute certainty here: utility repair crews will not be dispatched to work in a pitch-dark environment besieged by falling molten rocks. A feeling of abject resignation and isolation will have seeped into the consciousnesses of the living, to remain at least for the duration of the "storm."

One shudders to consider what it would be like to be cut off from the outside world on Manhattan Island, if all the access bridges and tunnels were destroyed. It would be utter hell on Earth. Conversely, if one were living way out in the middle of nowhere, halfway between Las Vegas and Reno, the isolation factor would be a definite drawback. One's best chance of survival would be in a "suburban" type of area, near a larger city possibly, with ample means of escape by roadway. In the event of a lull in the storm, we might wish to try to seek out others in our nearby environs for consultation and cooperation. But even under the best of circumstances, we shall encounter death and destruction all around us. The dead will simply have to be left to decompose and stink where they lie, providing food for roving packs of dogs and other homeless vultures. The stench of the rotting dead will become the least important of our problems. (People in war-zones will tell you that if there are bloating corpses all around, try to breathe through a cloth soaked in isopropyl rubbing alcohol – assuming that you have any left.)

These electrical sparks between Nibiru and Earth will jolt our Planet to its very core, setting off worldwide earthquakes and volcanoes. Volcanic smoke and ash will fill the atmosphere, obscuring further our view of the Sun and sky; and that 4-day-long darkness described by Dr. Velikovsky will commence. If the lampfires of the ancients could not penetrate this heavy darkness, then will be able to see anything with our flashlights, assuming that the batteries still work? It will be a horrifying period even for those of us who are aware in advance of what to expect.

These electrical sparks will have the added effect of disrupting the ocean tides by causing the waters to "heap up" rather than ebb and flow as normal. Once this electrical phenomenon ends, these heaping waters will come crashing down in immense tidal waves against the world's seashores, washing away still thousands more of those who have survived thus far.

Robertino Solàrion

CHANNELED MESSAGE FROM DIANE OF SIRIUS

My Dear Ones there are stories circulating amongst you that are producing a wave of fear that could engulf the Earth if it remains unchecked or unchallenged. It revolves around Planet X that is referred to "as coming" towards your Solar System, and is going to cause untold death and destruction. Its arrival is viewed as imminent, and certain countries are alleged to have already started preparations in their defense. A picture is being painted of a Star Wars scenario, which is being encouraged by the dark forces. Can you not see that this is the last bold attempt being made, to undo all of the good work carried out by the Lightworkers? There are forces at work that seek to prevent your ongoing journey to Ascension.

I would ask you, do you really think that we would stand by and allow the path decreed for the end times to be assailed or changed by threats against the people of Earth? We of the Galactic Federation are your protectors, and have been your galactic parents ensuring that you become the Cosmic Beings that are your true destiny. Although we have defined lines of help that limit what would be seen as "interference" in your self determination and freedom of choice, we have responsibility for the greater plan of this Universe. Even if the threat of Planet X were real, it would have been prevented from entering this Solar System. There is the Creator's Plan for the completion of your journey in duality, and it cannot be changed or usurped by any member of the dark forces.

Let us put your minds at rest, and inform you that Planet X is already in your Solar System, and the reason it has been allowed is because it no longer poses any threat to you or planet Earth. The Annunaki have had a history of presenting themselves as Gods, and leading man into the darkness by playing upon his lower vibrations.

Out Of The Darkness – UFO Revelations And Planet X

That period subsequently led to hundreds of years of conflict right up to the latter part of the last century. However, they were shown how they could help you out of your descent into total destruction, and at the same time settle some of the karmic debts they owed you. After all, the cycle of duality is destined to end soon, and with or without their help it would have been achieved. Now they wait hidden away in a location behind the Sun, to return to Earth at an appropriate time to atone for their actions and undo the harm they caused. Let it be said that the vibration upon Earth attracted them in the first place, and they fulfilled Man's search for the Gods that gave their favors to those who supported them, and cause their "enemies" to be smitten.

There is no longer a need for a violent end time as imagined by those who believe in Armageddon, and whilst it was possible before the end of the last century, that time has passed. The Light has awakened the consciousness of great numbers of you, so much so that you have changed the end time reality. The Supreme God of this Universe does not take sides, and loves each and every one of his/her souls without any judgment whatsoever. You can now lay aside those biblical stories that tell of the false Gods, who have pitted Man against Man. It is also time to leave behind those prophesies that were relevant until Man rose up into the higher consciousness, out of the darkness to create the opportunities that now lead to Ascension.

You may wonder how it is that so many realities exist side by side, and it is because Man has created them with such great energies that they have become powerful thought forms in their own right. You attach yourself to one by choice, and for you it becomes your reality. The dark feed those that serve their purpose, by continuing to play upon your fears. However, you are entering a new era on the path of Light breaking your ties with the past. Now you are clearing your karma and experiencing the great cleansing of Earth, as all preparations are being made that will enable your upliftment, never to return to this cycle of duality.

Times are rapidly changing but people are still sensitive to the negative energies, but they must not be allowed to take you away from the new path of Light you have created. The dark are in their death throes, and are lashing out to create chaos and fear as a last attempt to divert your attention from your goal. You are being subjected to fear laden predictions, and it is essential more than ever before that you stay focused on the Light. Trust your intuition, and know that your guides come near to you at this important time, and will impress you with the truth if you so allow them. The remaining months of this year are vital to your future, and should herald the first major changes that will ensure your victory over the dark forces. We do not believe for one moment that you will succumb to the attempts being made to entrap you, ones that lead you into believing the lies and misinformation that are meant to take your attention away from the pathway of Light. However, the energies of fear are disrupting and upsetting, that if you are not focused they can open you up so that you are susceptible to them.

There is a battle between the dark and Light, but you have the advantage of being able to deflect the lower energies by firmly staying in your Love and Light. It is the most powerful force in the Universe, and your help is needed to send it out to those who falter and in their uncertainty become lost in the whirlpool of mixed emotions. Fear as we have often informed you is the weapon of the dark, and they feed upon it to still try and advance their plans for total control of Earth. It will fail and is collapsing, taking its leaders with it and very soon the truth will become more widely known as to how you have been manipulated and used to fulfill their ambitions.

The Earth is beginning to "shake" out the negative energies as it reforms its body, and it is unavoidably necessary. However, we unbeknown to you lessen the effect to keep damage and loss of life to a minimum. Suddenly the more emphatic changes will quiet down, and with First Contact coming near we will be able to interact with you all the more. If necessary we shall temporarily move you to safe areas until the more physical changes are completed. Do not however worry about the souls that are passing on, as they will be treated with great love and tenderness to quickly release the experience of their trauma. They will have no regrets as they learn that they were part of their life contracts. You are immortal and have infinite life, and have spent hundreds of lives on your Earth. In the future you will not have need to experience death such as you understand it now, and you will move from one life to another with complete ease and in full consciousness.

I am Diane of Sirius and open my arms to bring you into our Light and Love, and have spoken to you on behalf of the Galactic Federation and the Spiritual Councils that oversee your evolution. They determine your path, so as to ensure its completion in accord with the greater plan of the Creator. Ride through the next few months with your eyes focused on the outcome, as out of the apparent chaos will come opportunities to leave the old behind, and bring the new into being. Believe in your highest concepts, and become that great Being of Light you really are and always have been and you will be contributing to the upliftment of Earth.

There is nothing to fear, and your evolutionary path is opening up for you. Soon the dark will be forced to give up its hold upon you, and then you shall see the Light in all its glory. This period of confusion will quickly pass, to allow a great coming together of the people of Earth in complete unity and purpose. You have strived long for this time, and now you will see the final acts played out as the dark forces are removed, and their influence no longer able to harm you. The energy of Love now pervades the Earth, and you are those who will ensure it is safely grounded. We are with you all of the way, and our help is at your call and beckoning. We Are All One for Evermore.

Mike Quinsey

ENTERING OUR GALACTIC DAY

Many of us are aware of the Mayan calendar, but not everyone truly understands what it means and how it works. The Maya had a very precise understanding of our solar system's cycles and believed that these cycles coincided with our spiritual and collective consciousness.

The Maya prophesied that starting from 1999 we have only a certain amount of time to realize that we need to deviate from our path of self-destruction and move instead onto a path that opens our consciousness to integrate us with all that exists. The Maya knew that our sun, or Kinich-Ahau, every so often synchronized with the Milky Way galaxy. From this central galaxy there will be a "spark" of light or energy which will cause the sun to shine more intensely and produce massive solar flares and changes in the Sun's magnetic field. This also causes disruptions in the Earth's rotation, and because of this movement great catastrophes would occur. The Maya said that this happens every 5,125 years.

The Maya believed the universal processes, like the "breathing" of the galaxy, are cycles that never change. What changes is the consciousness of man that passes through it, always in a process toward more perfection. The sun, having received a powerful ray of synchronizing light from the center of the galaxy, will change its polarity which will produce a great cosmic event that will propel humankind into a new era, The Golden Age. It is after this, that the Maya says we will be ready to transform our civilization to a vibration much higher in harmony.

Only with our individual efforts can we avoid the path to great cataclysm that our planet will suffer during the next cycle of the sun. The Mayan civilization believed that each cycle was just one stage in the collective consciousness of humanity. In the last cataclysm of the Maya, the civilization was destroyed by a great flood that left few survivors. They believed that having known the end of their cycle, mankind would prepare for what is to come in the future. They say that coming changes will permit us to make a quantum leap forward in the evolution of our consciousness to create a new civilization that would manifest great harmony and compassion to all humankind.

Their first prophecy talks about "The Time of No-Time," a period of 20 years, from 1992 to after 2012, which they call a Katún. The Maya predicted that during these times, solar winds would become more intense and this will be a time of great realization and great change for mankind. As well, it will be our own lack of preservation and contamination of the planet that would contribute to these changes. According to the Maya, these changes will happen so that mankind comprehends how the universe works so we can advance to superior levels, leaving behind superficial materialism and liberating ourselves from suffering.

The Mayans say that seven years after the start of Katún, 1999, we entered a time of darkness which would force us to confront our own behavior. The say that this is the time when mankind will enter "The Sacred Hall of Mirrors" where we will look at ourselves and analyze our behaviors with ourselves, with others, with nature and with the planet in which we live.

It was prophesied that the start of this period would be marked by a solar eclipse on August 11, 1999, known to them as 13 Ahau, 8 Cauac. This coincided with an unprecedented planetary alignment, the "Grand Cross" alignment. This would be the last 13 years of the Katón period, and the last opportunity for our civilization to realize the changes that are coming at the moment of our spiritual regeneration.

As individuals we have to make decisions that will affect us all. If we continue on this negative path of hate, fear, egotism and destruction of nature, we will enter into the time of destruction and chaos and disappear as the dominant race on Earth. If we become conscious and realize that we are all part of Creation, then we will move directly into positive growth, our Golden Age. It is up to us what will happen in this time of change.

CHAPTER SEVEN
The New Dawn of Consciousness
By Diane Tessman

In the 26 years I have channeled my guide Tibus, he has not mentioned once that Planet X is on the way. In May 2003, Planet X was believed to be coming but Tibus said it was not. It did not come. Now the goal posts have been moved; Planet X is coming in 2012, it is said. Tibus assures us today that Planet X is not coming within the next 20 years.

Now, maybe Tibus is wrong, although his batting average on predictions is high. It is both his and my strong belief that we need not worry about Planet X. Perhaps this puts us at odds with other writers in this book, and we do not aim to disagree with them. However, it is good that different opinions are given, especially on such an earth-shaking subject. In fact, it is exactly how things should be.

The reader should not let himself be ruled by the fear that Planet X is looming but instead look into his own heart and soul, finding hope and enlightenment. Always use logic and reason, too. Never allow fear to rule! Not only is fear a bad feeling, it allows negative entities and energies to enter the individual; a doomsday reality can actually be created by allowing fear to dominate.

It is Tibus' teaching that Planet Earth is undergoing her Change Times. He tells us that every sentient planet reaches a critical moment in her history when huge changes ensue. There are violent natural upheavals in the form of earthquakes, volcanoes, super-storms, droughts, floods, radical climate-change all around, and there is usually a final crisis of nuclear war or weapons which the dominant species on the planet has foolishly developed and used. A planet in her Change Times eventually reaches the epitome of this extreme upheaval and crisis; this point is known as the Change Point. Some might call is Doomsday. The early 21st century is the most likely time for this Change Point to occur.

Diane Tessman at Harristown Dolmen in Magical Ireland.

Out Of The Darkness – UFO Revelations And Planet X

However, Tibus tells us that there is no such thing as doomsday, because there is no such thing as death, not for an individual, not for any living creature, and not for a planet. We never know death, we only know life. Consciousness radiates throughout the universe, trumping time and space. Consciousness spirals onward and upward infinitely, always changing and mutating into new life forms.

Planet Earth is a living, breathing being; we call her wonderful spirit, "Gaia." As Gaia reaches "doomsday" on her Change Times clock, she will not die, and she will evolve to a new, higher level of consciousness.

Planets reincarnate just as people do. There will be a New Earth! Tibus calls this New Earth, the New Dawn.

Sometimes Tibus uses the analogy of new software being placed in a computer, entirely changing the program. The old human program was a lower consciousness level, but the new human program is a high level of consciousness. It will be literally a different dimension. No more war, no more greed, no more cruelty toward other humans, toward other life forms, or toward our planet.

Humans, who have achieved a degree of enlightenment, will graduate with their planet to a higher realm wherein dwell our angel friends, good extraterrestrials, future humans, and a whole host of wondrous life forms. To use the software analogy, if the new program of higher consciousness can be used in your computer, you will have a wondrous new reality. You need only be gentle, peaceful, empathetic, and loving, because these are what make you enlightened! Humans are about to graduate from Homo sapiens to Homo cosmos.

Tibus has the following message regarding Planet X and what is about to happen:

This is Tibus. I come to you in love and light.

Hello, my friends. I wish to express that our approach, our mission, is and always has been, to not only prepare you for the huge changes that are coming, but to help you through to a much better dimension. To make it through, you need spiritual readiness.

Spirit alone is eternal. Spirit always springs up again, elsewhere/elsewhen. There is no death. In the past, Earth has needed enlightened souls in a dark dimension; enlightened humans have shown the way out of the Dark Ages and into the Renaissance, out of the fearful nuclear 1950s, into the Age of Aquarius. However, the coming graduation is the time when Gaia, the living spirit of Mother Earth, and her enlightened humans, will transition to a higher reality. Coming along also will be all the delightful and diverse life forms of Mother Earth, from cats to whales, from sparrows to lions. All will sing a higher song.

Ultimately, it makes little difference whether Planet X causes upheavals and destruction, or whether global warming causes newly freed methane gas to set the oceans afire, or whether melting ice sheets cause the waters to gobble up the land – the old mundane dimension is winding down! I have even heard the argument that the planet is getting colder, not warmer and if this might be the case, a new Ice Age results in the same. All is about to Change with a capital "C."

However, this is not a fearful event but a joyous one. You will continue and flourish, singing a higher song.

All dimensions eventually wind down and fade into oblivion, but a new dimension always springs up. Life incarnates! The spiral is always upward.

Therefore, it is our belief, our approach, not to dwell on negative threats and fears. Who cares what the New World Order is doing in the way of underground bunkers to "save" its greedy, evil self? We do not dwell in the latest theory such as Planet X, 2003, or Planet X, whenever. This plays into the hands of fear, and fear will impede the journey of an individual as he travels to the New Dawn.

If there is such a thing as Planet X (and we do not believe there is), it will hit Old Earth. New Earth is not of Old Earth's time line; in fact, New Earth is beyond the chains of time entirely. If you should "die" because of Planet X, you as an enlightened soul, will spring up again in a world of higher consciousness which has no physical connection to the events which just happened on Old Earth. Your enlightened spirit will take you to the New Dawn anyway.

There is simply nothing to be gained from dwelling on the fear of what is coming (or not!). You are a good soul, full of love and compassion despite what the old world may have dealt you. The New Dawn awaits you. At the Change Point, science and spirit will come together and enhance each other. On Old Earth, they are perceived as contradictory. If you are scientifically inclined, please listen to my words as well, this is not "just" about spirit. This is about reality itself, as much born of quantum physics as metaphysics.

All things in creation have a spiritual aspect and a scientific aspect. The dimension of the New Dawn is spiritually inspiring because it is composed of a higher level of consciousness particle; the New Dawn is the hope of a risen world. Metaphysics has always told us that hope, inspiration, will power, positive meditation, and unconditional love, have real power which can create reality.

However, this higher level of consciousness particle is also solid quantum physics. Consciousness travels on sub-atomic particles and indeed, is composed of sub-atomic particles. Therefore, the coming dimensional shift on Earth is not a religious belief at all. It is something that will happen due to the nature of universal quantum physics. When enough enlightened minds are awakened in these Change Times, the critical mass of enlightenment will occur. Mass consciousness functions at a specific hum; that hum can be raised an octave when there are enough like-minds and like-spirits.

I assure you that it will only take tens of thousands of awakened, enlightened minds for this critical mass to occur and shift the dimension upward. It will not take billions or even millions of people. Every day in these Change Times, more humans become enlightened, and the Change Point draws near. It may well come in after the year 2012.

It is easy to miss the entire point about these Change Times.

This is the moment for the human race to evolve.

This is the moment for the human race to take responsibility. It is the moment for the human race to grow up!

To believe Planet X is coming, takes one's focus from what is really happening. To believe Planet X is coming, makes one miss the big chance to evolve spiritually, thus saving oneself and Planet Earth with all her wondrous life forms. It must come from within! Planet X is the outside bogey man about which one can do nothing. It must be asked; perhaps someone deliberately wants to take away your awesome power by diverting your focus to a frightening scenario.

What do I mean by "humankind must take responsibility?"

No one can deny what the human race has done to Earth's rivers, oceans, forests, wet lands; no one can deny how many birds, animals, and plants, stand on the brink of oblivion because of human cruelty, insensitivity, and greed. No one can deny that humans have made war on each other, on women and children, on the land, on its life forms, for millennia. Unspeakable suffering and anger have occurred because of war. Humankind is the primary reason for drastic, sudden climate-change, whether it amounts to global warming or global cooling. All was in balance and would have stayed this way for thousands of years. Old Earth is dying much too early a death.

Enlightenment (salvation!) dawns as more and more humans take responsibility to love and care for their Mother Planet, her life forms, and each other. It is really so wonderfully simple! Enlightenment is therefore a logical thing as much as a spiritual thing.

Over-involvement in a doomsday scenario, chains you to that scenario, it chains you to the emotion of fear, and it is fear which hinders spiritual evolution, manifesting negative entities and energies. In short, you will be stuck in the unenlightened hum of Old Earth.

Keep your eye on the highest star, the best goal where hope lives. Of course you should explore various theories and scenarios', always remembering that fear makes money, taking away your power and handing it to others.

Is the Mayan Year of The End actually the Change Point? It is very likely.

The reality continuum flows freely and spontaneously, like small streams into the larger river. We explain the "reality continuum" concept in our book Earth Changes Bible. I cannot tell you precisely which "little stream" you are in until "it" happens. We do know the Change Point is bound to happen in a few short years.

That moment is not written in stone, the future is always open, not closed. However, these are the Change Times of Mother Earth and the moment of dimensional shift will happen soon, just as the Mayans foresaw. They simply did not see, or could not describe in words, the reality beyond that incredible moment; thus it is interpreted that they saw The End of Days.

A quantum leap is coming when humankind will no longer be Homo sapiens but instead, an enlightened new race called Homo cosmos. Humans in the New Dawn will function on this higher hum of mass consciousness.

At the Change Point, a new door of reality will open, a new dimension will form and be solidified in reality. You will perceive it, you will be it!

MAY THE HEALING LIGHT OF GOODNESS SURROUND YOU, ALWAYS.

Diane Tessman would love to hear from you! Receive a packet of free literature; send only $5.00 to cover postage.

Address:
Diane Tessman
P.O. Box 352
St. Ansgar, Iowa, 50472

E-mail: dtessman@iowatelecom.net
Web site: www.DianeTessman.com

Ask Diane about the five books she and her guide Tibus have written, receive a free Heartline newsletter and a free 20 page Change Times Quarterly with urgent warnings and predictions! Act now!

CHAPTER EIGHT
How To Survive The Changing Times

Earthquake in China, cyclones in Burma, hurricanes, tornadoes, wildfires, all of this remind us that disasters are part of the human condition. We are more or less vulnerable to them no matter where we live. It doesn't matter if Planet X will or will not arrive anytime soon. It doesn't matter that the planets poles could shift, or if a massive shockwave from the center of the galaxy strikes us head on. We live in very trying times; gas has become almost unaffordable to a large portion of the populations; food is becoming scarce; our homes are being taken away from us and the government seems to be totally helpless, or unwilling to take charge and try to fix things.

This means that we cannot depend on anyone else to help us when things get bad. We have to know how to help ourselves.

Survival is not just a product of luck. We can do far more than we think to improve our odds of preventing and surviving even the most horrendous of catastrophes. It's a matter of preparation – bolting down your water heater before an earthquake or actually reading the in-flight safety card before takeoff – but also of mental conditioning. Each of us has a "disaster personality," a state of being that takes over in a crisis. It is at the core of who we are. The fact is, we can refine that personality and teach our brains to work more quickly, maybe even more wisely.

Humans are programmed with basic survival skills. When frightened, we get a shot of performance-enhancing hormones, and the blood pumps to our limbs to help us outrun whatever enemy we face. But in modern times, we're hardly aware of such natural skills, and most of us do little to understand or develop them.

We could, for example, become far better at judging threats before catastrophe strikes. We have technological advantages that our ancestors lacked, and we know where disasters are likely to occur. And yet we flirt shamelessly with risk. We construct city skylines in hurricane alleys and neighborhoods on top of fault lines

– as if nature will be cowed by our audacity and leave us be. And we rely on a sprawling network of faraway suppliers for necessities like warmth and food. If the power cuts off, many of us still don't know where the stairs are in our skyscrapers, and we would have trouble surviving for a week without the local big discount store. For many people, preparation means little more than crossing their fingers and hoping to live.

Yet the knowledge is out there. Risk experts understand how we could overcome our blind spots and more intelligently hedge our bets. In laboratories and on shooting ranges, there are people who study what happens to bodies and minds under extreme duress. Police, soldiers, race-car drivers and helicopter pilots train to anticipate the strange behaviors they will encounter at the worst of times. Regular people can learn from that knowledge, since, after all, we will be the first on the scene of any disaster.

Of course, no one can promise a plan of escape. But that doesn't mean we should live in willful ignorance. As Hunter S. Thompson said, "Call on God, but row away from the rocks."

HOW TO SURVIVE REALLY HARD TIMES

In the old days, folks were accustomed to periodically having to live through hard times. They knew how to survive the hard times with the least amount of wear and tear on their families. Nowadays, most people don't know what hard times really are. Even those who think they have it hard right now can usually still depend on some type of government handout or charity and therefore they don't really know what hard times are all about.

One thing that really needs to be driven home is that we cannot expect the government to help us out when things really get bad. Take a look at what happened to New Orleans after hurricane Katrina. People were dying in the streets and the President got on TV and said things were under control. Well they were not. The government botched things up badly and then tried to cover up their mistakes by trying to manipulate the media into painting a rosy picture over what was really going on. This was the same technique they used to fool the American public into believing that war with Iraq was a necessity for their safety. Fortunately, the truth got out and people all over the world realized just how bad it was in Louisiana and just how useless the United States government really was in handling a disaster.

You are better off depending on yourself, your family and your local community then in depending on your government to save you. This means to make the types of decisions and preparations with the thought in mind that no one else is going to help you when things get really rough.

My definition of hard times is when things are not what they use to be and they don't look like they will return to normal anytime soon. This frequently happens in times of war, economic collapse, floods, tornadoes, hurricanes and other unexpected disasters. Often, these types of disasters are usually accompanied by power failures that last for days, weeks, or months.

One of the first rules of survival is to stay where you are. This is important unless your home is threatened or damaged to the point that it is more dangerous then venturing out. During perilous times, you don't need to get wet, cold, frost bitten, or endangered by hostile individuals.

There is no building that is completely 100% safe from all threats. But you can do a lot to make your home as safe as possible. Make sure all of your doors leading to the outside have deadbolts on them. As well, get locks for your windows. Nothing is going to keep someone out who is determined to get in. But, anything that you can do to make this as difficult as possible is going to work in your favor.

This is why the community is going to be important. Individuals are going to be worse off than the community as a whole. When things get bad, your community is going to have to come together in cooperation. Remember when Hillary Clinton said that it takes a village to raise a child. She was given a lot of grief over this statement, but she is correct, and not just with raising children. It takes a village to insure survival. The sharing of food, protection, work, rebuilding etc. is going to be the key factor on whether or not you and your neighbors are going to survive.

In the event of a worldwide disaster fuel shortages will precipitate shortages of food, medicine, and countless consumer items, outages of electricity, gas, and water, breakdowns in transportation systems and other infrastructure, hyperinflation, widespread shutdowns and mass layoffs, along with a lot of despair, confusion, violence, and lawlessness.

The U.S. population is almost entirely dependent on their cars and relies on markets that control oil importation, refining, and distribution. They also rely on continuous public investment in road construction and repair. Also motor vehicles require a steady stream of imports of both parts and whole vehicles neither of which is designed to last very long. When these intricately inter-dependent systems stop functioning the bulk of the U.S. population will be virtually immobilized as public transport systems are negligible.

Families generally tend to be atomized, geographically dispersed and unused to sharing. Families unused to sharing in good times are likely to find it very difficult to co-operate in bad times. Competitiveness and personal isolation tend to be endemic already and a collapse because of disaster is unlikely to cure these attitudes and situations. A major disaster tends to shut down both local production and imports, and so it is vitally important that anything you own wears out slowly, and that you or someone in your family or community (if you have one to call on) can fix it if it breaks.

In the U.S. most people get their food from a supermarket, which is supplied from far away using refrigerated diesel trucks. Many people also eat fast food. When people do cook, they rarely cook from scratch. Apart from being unhealthy, these habits will cease to be viable if super markets and fast food sellers are unable to get food supplies from distant places.

WATER

Without water, a person will dehydrate and start to die in about three days. This first step to survival in hard times is to inventory your water into two categories: drinking water and all other water. If the water is on, fill all the water containers you have in the house (anything that will hold water and not leak). This includes your bathtubs. If the water is off, be creative. Ice cubes in the freezer; water inside the hot water heater. Both are safe to drink.

Water that isn't safe to drink is toilet bowl water and water inside the mattress of a water bed. However, the water in your toilet tank is safe to drink.

Many canned foods are packed in water. When you open a can, serve the water in the can with the food (don't throw the canned water away if you are low on water). The second step to survival in hard times is to ration your water. During normal times, one person needs one gallon of water per day. During hard times, a person can survive for a short period of time on two quarts of water per day (two quarts is one-half gallon). If water is really in short supply, then one quart per day will keep a person alive, but they will begin to slowly dehydrate.

Everyone knows better, but after a long period of little or no water, a person will drink all the water they can when it suddenly becomes available in quantity. If you do this, you will get sick. Drink one cup of water every 15 minutes. Give your system a chance to absorb the water and send it where it is needed most. Don't overload your system or you will kill yourself.

When your water runs low, where can you get more? Collect rain water. If you have rain gutters on your dwelling, use rain barrels to capture the rain at the end of the down spouts. A good thunderstorm can provide more than enough water for you and your family.

Be creative. Think about what you have available that you can put outside to catch and store rain water. Remember that it usually rains one inch or less every time it rains. You need a large surface area to collect enough rain water to drink. A small cup or glass won't do. Even a five gallon cook pot is too small to just put outside by itself (it will only collect 1 inch of water in the bottom of the pot). Something like a child's plastic swimming pool would be ideal. You can even put clean bed sheets outside your windows, let them get drenched in rain, ring them out by hand inside the house into a pot, and stick them back out in the rain again.

If it doesn't rain, go outside at dawn and collect the morning dew. One good method is to dig a shallow hole and put a bucket or pot in the center. Next, line the hole with a sheet of plastic so it makes a funnel shape into the bucket. Cut a hole in the bottom of the plastic over the bucket. As the dew collects on the plastic, it will run down the sides and drip into the bucket. A number of these scattered all over your property will collect enough water to survive the day. You can also collect morning dew by soaking a cloth in long, wet grass. When the cloth is soaked wring it out directly into your mouth or a container.

You can also use your plastic to make a solar still. This is a wilderness survival technique for gathering water in very dry locations, especially in the desert where finding water can be difficult. There are two essential components – a container to catch the water and a plastic sheet.

The basic principle is that solar energy heats the soil in a hole by passing through a plastic sheet. Moisture from the soil then evaporates, causing condensation to form on the plastic. Make sure when you are selecting your site for your still you look for a sunny location.

Dig a hole about three ft wide and two ft deep. You can use the hole you have already dug to collect dew. Again, make sure it is in a sunny location.

Place a collecting can or bucket at the bottom. Cover the hole with a plastic sheet formed into a cone and hold it in place with rocks. Make sure you use a section of the plastic that does not have the hole you cut into it for dew collection.

Place a small rock onto the plastics center so the lowest point of the plastic sheet is directly above the container. The sun will raise the temperature of the air and soil in the hole, producing vapor. Moisture will condense on the underside of the plastic sheet and water will drop into the container. At the end of the day, remove the plastic to collect the water. If constructed correctly, your solar still can yield about a quart of water a day.

Tree and plants roots draw moisture from the ground. Use that fact to collect water without digging. Tie a plastic bag over a growing branch with exposure to the sun. Be careful and don't puncture the bag. Close the bag and keep a corner hanging low to collect water. Evaporation from the leaves will produce condensation in the bag. This is an easy way to get pure drinkable water.

Ground water is usually the most contaminated. Ground water is lake, pond, creek, stream, or river water if you live in the country. In the city, it is water flowing beside the sidewalks during a heavy rain. If no other source of water is available, then you may be forced to collect the only water you can find. But do not drink it until you purify it. Even if the water looks crystal clear in a glass, it can still contain tiny organisms that will make you sick. You don't need a severe case of diarrhea or a high fever during hard times. Like the old saying goes, it is better to be safe than sorry.

To purify water, first, pour the water through a standard paper coffee filter (or clean pillow case). This will trap and remove any large impurities. The same coffee filter can be used over and over again for a long time, unless the water is very muddy or dirty.

After you have pre-filtered your water, you can use one of the following three options to purify the water:

1. Boil the water at a hard boil for about 10 minutes. Wait for the water to cool. Then pour the water from one container into another container several times to add air back into the water to improve its taste.

2. Or put two drops of chlorine liquid bleach (unscented) in each quart of water and wait one hour for the bleach to kill all the tiny organisms. (Or eight drops per gallon.)

3. As a last result, you can put three drops of iodine (2 % strength) into each quart of water and wait one hour. (Or 12 drops per gallon.)

If there is snow or ice on the ground, you can collect it and melt it inside your house. Never melt the snow or ice inside your mouth. This consumes more water than you get back in return (water vapor lost through your mouth and nose while breathing). You dehydrate more quickly and end up worse off than when you started. If necessary, you can put the snow inside a small container and put the capped container inside your clothing (but not next to your skin) and your body heat will gradually melt the snow into water. If you are concerned about the cleanliness of the snow, then you can boil the resulting water 10 minutes before you drink it.

If you are short on water, do not waste it bathing or washing your clothes. Just wash your hands and face periodically. Don't discard the water until it is too dirty to use again. Wash your dishes in one pot of water with dish soap. Rinse the dishes in a second pot.

Rinse the dishes again in a third pot. When the dish water in the first pot gets really nasty, discard it. Then put dish soap in the second pot and use it as the initial wash pot. Use the third pot as your first rinse. And add a new pot with clean water as the final rinse. If your sewer is still working properly, you can pour your waste water down your toilet to flush it.

HEAT

During cold weather you need to stay warm. In the days before central heating, people felt comfortable in their houses during the winter if the temperature was 40 degrees or warmer. This was because they wore warm clothes inside the house. They knew that several thin layers of clothing felt warmer than one or two thick garments. There is a layer of air between each layer of clothing and that air forms a pocket of insulation to help retain your body heat. If a person got too warm, they would take off one layer of clothing and they would cool off and be comfortable again.

People would also wear hats inside the house during the winter. When a person is normally dressed, they lose 90% of their body heat through their head. So to stay warm, wear a hat.

Close all of your windows properly. This includes making sure storm windows are down if you have them. Windows should be latched. Open them during the day if the outside temperature is higher than the inside.

Keep your windows air-tight. You may want to purchase removable window-caulk or plastic to better seal them. At a minimum, stuff a towel, a sheet, or shirt in front of any noticeable leaks.

Use cheap clear shower curtains over the windows that receive sun light. This will keep the cold air out, and the warmth from the sun will heat your house without cold air coming in.

If your home is still too cold for you (below 40 degrees), then you need to reduce the size of your living area. If you have a big closet, then move the family into it. If all your rooms are big, then partition off one corner of one room using mattresses to make temporary walls. In other words, build a small temporary room in the corner of a big room. Use all your extra sheets and blankets to insulate this smaller living area. Remember, heat rises. Therefore, let fresh air into your living space somewhere down close to the floor.

This will enable the body heat to increase the temperature of a smaller area by 10 to 15 degrees. In addition, each time someone exhales, their breath will also contribute to an increase in the temperature of the small area. This technique works. The Inuit's live in a frozen wasteland and they survive year after year. This is because they build small igloos that capture and conserve their body heat.

Candles can also be used to generate heat in a small area. Just be mindful of where they are placed and do not leave them unattended. Stock up on candles; make sure that you have plenty on hand. In my opinion, you can never have too many candles.

If you have a wood burning fireplace or wood stove, use it for heat if possible; save your propane or fuel oil for a real emergency. Bring in enough firewood once per day so you don't keep opening and closing the door and let the heat escape. If you do not have a chimney, do not start a fire inside. The smoke will kill you. Even if you build the fire near a window, the smoke will gradually fill your dwelling. And you will lose any heat from the fire through the window.

SELF-PROTECTION

There is only one sure way to win a fight. Avoid it. Avoid fights with other people, and stray dogs, and wild animals. Avoid fights by staying inside your house. If you must go outside, try to blend in with your environment (whatever it happens to be at the time), and don't attract attention to yourself. Speak softly. Move quietly and slowly. Most people won't attack a person who is visible armed (pistol in holster or hunting knife on waist belt). Don't carry a weapon in your hand. You would be advertising that you are either looking for trouble or that you are afraid. Neither is a good sign if you are trying to blend in.

On the other hand, if you are backed into a corner and no option is left except to fight, then fight to win. Use whatever weapons are convenient at the time.

This is where the concept of the village also comes in handy. If your community has joined together in mutual cooperation, then handling dangerous and threatening elements becomes a community challenge, not just yours alone. Remember, it is safest during times of crisis to be part of a larger group.

Also, if you choose to use firearms, either as protection or for hunting, always have a stockpile of ammunition and spare parts for each weapon. This is a problem with firearms, eventually you are going to run out of shells, so think ahead.

FOOD

First rule, if you have no water to drink, then don't eat. Second rule, remember the first rule when you get really hungry.

Your body uses water to digest food, and if you eat without drinking any liquids, then your body will draw the water it needs to digest the food from your body tissues and you will dehydrate and die much faster. A person can go three weeks without food, but three days without water and you are dead. Never forget the first rule.

If you believe it may be some time before you can replenish your food supplies, then inventory all the food in your home and begin rationing on day one. Inventory your food based on the major food groups and on the number of calories listed on the label on each box or can. If you have food in the refrigerator, and the power is off, then eat it before you start on your canned foods.

Here is a tip to keep your refrigerated and frozen foods longer without electricity. Fill empty milk jugs with water and freeze them in your freezer. When the electricity goes out, take these jugs and store as many as you can in your refrigerator. This will keep your foods cold longer, especially if you minimize the amount of times you open the door. Don't forget to keep some in your freezer as well. These jugs will also supply you with fresh drinking water when they unfreeze.

Eat refrigerator food first, then freezer food, and eat canned and boxed food last. After you have a list of all your food, plan a daily menu based on the order in which you intend to consume your food so you work all the major food groups strategically into your diet on a regular basis. Deviate from that plan if a particular food item looks like it might go bad if you save it any longer. Better to have the calories stored inside your body than to let them go to waste.

Speaking of waste, during hard times there is no excuse to throw away any food that is edible. Save all uneaten food. If it cannot be saved for the next meal, then someone should eat it while it is still edible because you never know when you will get to eat again.

If you have canned food, try to keep it from freezing which will rupture the can and ruin the food. Most canned foods remain edible after two or three years. Canned meat will last even longer. Therefore, don't worry about your canned food going bad if you purchased it during the previous year. After two or three years, the food will still be edible, but the taste and nutritional value of the food will be less. Drink the liquid inside canned food. It contains vitamins, fluids, and oils your body needs.

People in the U.S. eat over 2,500 calories a day. If you remain inactive you won't need that many calories to stay alive. A person can survive a long time on 1,000 calories per day if they remain relatively inactive.

If your food supply starts to run low, and the hard times look like they are not going to end soon, then cut back the calories to 750 per day. Most people will not suffer any permanent damage just because they continuously feel hungry.

If you have any vitamins in the house, ration them out to your family members. Each person should get two vitamin pills each week. The vitamins will last a long time this way, and each person will have a much better chance of staying healthy and not getting sick.

FOOD FROM NATURE

Wildlife: If you live near an area with trees, you may be able to get fresh squirrel or rabbit meat with a 22 rifle or a really good BB gun at close range. However, if you fry or roast the squirrel or rabbit, its meat it will be too tough to eat. Skin the animal, remove and discard the digestive organs (stomach and intestines), and cut the meat into small pieces (cut the heart and liver into pieces also), and boil all the meat in a little water with a dash of salt. This extends the meat so that more people can get something to eat at the same time.

Thin Evergreen Needles (pine, spruce, etc.): Those thin green needles are edible and are an excellent source of vitamin C. If you eat them year round you will notice they taste different during the different seasons. Sometimes the taste is neutral and sometimes a little bitter. Regardless of how they taste, they are still an edible food source. Remember, they are very low in calories, so they won't provide the energy you need – but they will provide some fresh natural vitamins. Pine needles may be eaten raw or cooked. Or you can dice the pine needles into very tiny pieces and boil them in some water to make a broth or tea.

Pine Cone Seeds: The seeds of a pine cone are located under the outer scales of the pine cone. Break off the scales to get to the seeds. There will be two winged seeds under each scale.

The seeds may be eaten raw, or you may roast them. This is one of the most important wild food sources due to its high food value and availability.

Soft Inner Tree Bark (not the hard outer bark): In the spring when the sap is rising, the inner bark of most trees is edible (pine, birch, elm, maple, spruce, willow). It is low in calories but better than nothing. Peel the bark up near the bottom of the tree or from exposed roots to reveal the fresh inner bark. Do not peel the bark off a tree in a circle all the way around the tree. You will kill the tree. Don't overdo it on a single tree. Move on to the next tree. Inner tree bark may be eaten raw, or cooked, or dried and pounded into flour for future consumption.

Dandelions: Most folks think of them as weeds. But, every part of the dandelion plant is edible (flower, stems, leaves, and roots). The stems and flowers can be eaten raw or cooked. The leaves taste bitter if eaten raw so it is usually better to boil them first. Remove the tough center vein from the leaves before you boil them. Wash the roots and boil them like a potato. Or you can dry the roots in the sun, crush them and use them as a substitute for coffee. From a medicinal perspective, any and all the parts of the dandelion plant help to improve blood circulation in the body as well as being good for the liver and digestion.

Clover: All types of clover are edible. Clover contains some vitamin E. Clover can be recognized by its small round flowers and its three small leaves. The clover leaves may be eaten raw or boiled (older leaves are better boiled). The tiny flowers can be boiled to make a tea. The roots can be scraped, washed, and boiled.

Bugs: Don't forget insects as a great source of protein. People from all over the world regularly eat bugs and have come up with all kinds of different ways to prepare them. They may be eaten raw (but not alive) or cooked. The best solution is to dice them into small pieces and cook them in a soup with some other type of wild food. Grasshoppers and crickets can also be eaten if you first remove the legs. The legs contain tiny barbs that can get caught in your throat. Don't eat grasshoppers raw because they occasionally contain tiny parasites which will be killed if you first boil the grasshoppers in water. Never eat flies, mosquitoes, ticks, centipedes, or spiders.

Depending on where you live, other edible foods may grow wild. Familiarize yourself with your local environment and study what Mother Nature has available to those in the know. Don't eat anything, plant, bug, animal unless you know for sure it is safe.

This is especially true of mushrooms. Unless you know for sure that it is safe, it is best to leave all mushrooms alone.

TOILET FACILITIES

If the water is off and the toilets don't work, then you will have to manually deal with human waste. Take two trash cans and line each one with two plastic trash can liner bags. When possible, put solid and liquid waste in separate containers. This allows the solids to dry out. Put something over the trash cans when they are not being used. You can urinate and defecate wherever it is comfortable for you, but pour the waste material into the trash cans. Periodically empty the trash cans. Don't just throw the waste outside. It will attract flies and other vermin that breed and spread disease. The best solution is to bury the waste underground.

If it looks like it is going to be a long time before your water is going to come back on, then you might have to make an outhouse. This is a very simple operation; dig a deep hole, about four feet deep and build a simple outhouse over the hole. Make sure that you keep your outhouse away from any water source. Keep a bucket of dirt inside the outhouse to throw a little dirt into the hole every time you use it. You will also need some lime to occasionally throw into the hole to keep the odor down.

When the hole gets full, move the outhouse, fill the hole with dirt and move to a different location. Mark the old hole so you don't accidentally dig there anytime soon.

A different type of waste problem is when the sewer works but you are short on water. That happens sometimes in the country with folks who have septic tanks but their water well goes dry (or almost dry). When that happens, you don't flush as often. You still use the stool all day long, but you only flush solid waste. To quote an old rhyme: "If it's yellow, let it mellow. If it's brown, flush it down."

EDUCATE YOURSELF BEFORE IT IS TOO LATE

- Learn to grow your own food, or at least a significant portion of it.

- Learn a trade skill that has true persistent need in any economy.

- Learn to make your own bread.

- Learn to can your own produce.

- Learn to raise chickens to supply your family with eggs and meat.

- Learn how to fix and maintain bicycles and motorbikes and scooters.

- Learn how to live without "services" to perform everything for you from fixing your bagel and coffee in the morning to fixing your method of transportation.

- Learn how to live on vastly less resources. Water, Electricity, Gas, Oil, etc.

- Learn how to do your own research, and then share what you learn with others.

Hard times bring out either the best or the worst in each of us. If you, you're family, and your community face hard times together sometime during your life, what kind of example do you want to set for your loved ones? In future years, when your children grow up and look back on the hard times, what do you want them to remember?

CHAPTER NINE
An E-Mail From A Norwegian Politician

The Conspiracy Journal newsroom received the following e-mail in January of 2008 claiming to be from a Norwegian politician with an incredible story to tell concerning 2022. Other groups that have received this e-mail have maintained contact with the sender and feel that this is not a hoax. I will leave it up for the reader to decide for themselves whether this e-mail has any validity or not.

I am a Norwegian politician. I would like to say that difficult things will happen from the year 2008 till the year 2022.

The Norwegian government is building more and more underground bases and bunkers. When asked, they simply say that it is for the protection of the people of Norway. When I enquire when they are due to be finished, they reply "before 2021."

Israel is also doing the same and many other countries too.

My proof that what I am saying is true is in the photographs I have sent of myself and all the Prime Ministers and ministers I tend to meet and am acquainted with. They know all of this, but they don't want to alarm the people or create mass panic.

Planet X is coming, and Norway has begun with storage of food and seeds in the Svalbard area and in the arctic north with the help of the US and EU and all around in Norway. They will only save those that are in the elite of power and those that can build up again: doctors, scientists, and so on.

As for me, I already know that I am going to leave before 2022 to go the area of Mosjøen where we have a deep underground military facility. There we are divided into sectors, red, blue and green. The signs of the Norwegian military are already given to them and the camps have already been built a long time ago.

The people that are going to be left on the surface and die with along the others will get no help whatsoever. The plan is that 2,000,000 Norwegians are going to be safe, and the rest will die. That means 2,600,000 will perish into the night not knowing what to do.

All the sectors and arks are connected with tunnels and have railcars that can take you from one ark to the other. This is so that they can be in contact with each other. Only the large doors separate them so that the sectors are not compromised in any matter.

I am very sad. Often I cry with others that know that so many will learn too late, and then it will all be over for them. The government has been lying to the people from 1983 till now. All the major politicians know this in Norway, but few will say it to the people and the public – because they are afraid in case they too will miss the NOAH 12 railcars that will take them to the ark sites where they will be safe.

If they tell anyone, they are dead for sure. But I don't care any more about myself. Mankind must survive and the species must survive. People must know this.

All the governments in the world are aware of this and they just say it is going to happen. For those of the people that can save themselves I can only say reach for higher ground and find caves up in the high places where you can have a food storage for at least five years with canned food and water to last for a while. Radiation pills and biosuits are also advisable if your budget allows it.

For the last time I say may God help us all... but God will not help us I know. Only each person individually can make a difference. Wake up, please...!

I could have written to you using another name but I am not afraid of anything any more. When you know certain things, you become invincible and no harm can come to you when you know that the end is soon.

I assure you 100% that things will happen. There are four years to prepare for the endgame. Get weapons, and make survival groups, and a place where you can be safe with food for a time. Ask me anything and I will answer as much as I know about the Norwegian connection to all this. And just look around:

they are building underground bases and bunkers everywhere. Open your eyes, people. Ask the governments what they are building, and they will say "Oh, it's just storage for food," and so on. They blind you with all the lies.

The marks of the alien presence are also there, and I often see the Norwegian elite politicians are not what they say they are. It's like they are controlled in every thought, and what they have to say is just as they are told to do things in such manners. It is clear for me who they are, and who they are not. You can see it in their eyes and in their minds.

Remember that those who are going to be in and around the city areas in 2022 are those that are going to be hit first and die first. Later the army will purge the rest of the survivors and they have a shoot to kill order if there is any resistance to bring them into the camps where every one will get marked with a number and a tag.

The public will not know what happens till the very end, because the government does not want to create mass panic. Everything will happen quietly and the government will just disappear.

But I say this: don't go quietly into the night. Take precautions to be safe with your family. Come together with others. Work together to find ways to solve all the many problems you will face.

Kind regards

(Name withheld)

The good people at Projectcamelot.net addressed a number of questions to the alleged politician, and received this response.

I have been to several underground bases [number given]. We used the railcars to get around. Only a few special people were selected to be shown around. Those that run with the elite know of this.

I have evidence of my claims. I trust my sources 100%, but they are afraid to tell what they know. People are afraid for their lives and that is how it is. I just also want the public to know what the hell is going on. I am not afraid of death or any other thing. All the elite politicians in Norway know of this. They also know that if they reveal anything they will be removed from office and will be denied access to the different underground bases when the time is up.

The NOAH 12 railcars are transport railcars between the different bases underground. They have a support system of these all around from one base to another. They are mainly used by the military and they control all of them. There are orange triangle symbols in each base and the check-ins are a kind of energy field that everyone has to go through.

The future for my children is all I think of - and that for all the other children growing up in the new world. We have to make a difference for them so that they grow up knowing what their parents did for them, such as giving this information to people like yourselves.

In 2009 the government of FRP will come into power and Siv Jensen will be elected Prime Minister. This is already known. It's important to understand that. The elections are all fake and the same persons and power elite get elected each time in turn. Look up the political history of Norway, and the people that run the country now.

Please share this information with the rest of the internet. When the time comes people will survive because of the information they have learned from the different sites on the net.

I will not get anything but trouble from posting this, and I have no need to mislead anyone. I do this only to expose what is to happen in my country and that maybe some people will survive what is to come.

When I was in the military I was in the [name of service given]. At one point we were given a task to get something out of a base and deliver it to another base.

We were told: "DO NOT ASK ANY QUESTIONS. JUST DO YOUR JOB." Later, when we landed outside the base, we were taken by trucks to outside the base where there were large doors heavily guarded by other military personnel.

Or it seemed like they were military, but they had different suits on them: orange and black suits with the orange suits having a golden triangle on them and the black suits having a green triangle.

As far as I can remember the triangle went downwards, like a pyramid but facing down and had some weird kind of sign on it. To me it looked like the letter 'E', but the lines were not connected in the 'E' like we write the letter 'E'. It was shaped like the 'E' and in the middle the letter 'E' was pointing inwards... not as in any language I can read or understand, and certainly not in Norwegian.

The signs were as far as I can remember not on the arms because I saw them clearly... they were at the left side of the black suit just over the chest area and on the caps they had on. The signs were not that big - just as a regular sized patch is, but clear enough to see them.

We went through the large doors. I was thinking what the hell this is, and I felt a bit scared at first. It was like something out of a science fiction movie. This was the first time I was in such a base.

We then came to a 500 meter long tunnel and there were more of these military personnel waiting with guns and transport for us. We were divided up in groups. Some went another way, and I and my group were asked to come with the black suited guards so they could take us to another location. When we came to the end we were asked to put on some masks "for our own protection."

I was thinking for our own protection... aren't we already protected by being inside this huge underground complex and by guards with weapons?

We were then asked to step inside a railcar... and this is what I know of the railcars. They are run by some kind of blue crystal energy, I think, or at least that is how it appeared. Then we sat in the cars and I asked one of the guards "What is this?" He replied, "You don't need to know this, sir."

At the front where the operator sits there was a box with a window just besides him, and just when before powering up you could see the large purple-blue crystals emitting a purple-bluish light... not blinding you but quite beautiful to watch indeed. I have never ever seen such energy light or crystals anywhere. I was thinking that must be the power source.

Later on in the base I saw that some people were working on these purple-blue crystals. They were larger than the ones I saw in the railcar - ca. one meter in length and they were lined up one after the other. They were taking some light through them. They were in fact purple-blue and when the light went inside they turned more blue and had a stronger color – the people had white masks on and goggles standing away from them when the light was going inside the crystals. I was about 20 meters from them and we were quickly rushed along when they said "Move on now."

I also think that the energy fields that we went through before entering the check-in were powered by these crystals, because it was the same kind of light - or so it seemed to me. If I remember more I will let you know. I could see that there was a tube-like system and the other railcars were just going so fast you just saw a light going by. I think this was a vacuum tube system where there is no drag.

The railcars were just like the tube itself but inside. The tube was a bit larger. The main car or transport shuttle was I think ca. 12 meters in length and had a pointed shape in front and back and had seating for 10 people with the operator. You could drive them both ways and it was not necessary to turn it around. It was sealed from the side after you go inside and was quite okay... but the speed was too much, and I got sick after the ride.

There was also some room for some cargo that you could take with you, but not much. There were a lot of these railcars around, as it seemed, and they just went passing by just like a light passes by in a flash. But you don't get to see the other rails either, because it's so fast that you forget to look and rather concentrate on your stomach when inside one of these.

Later on, after I went into politics, I found out what was inside of the rest of the base and what the bases are for, which I have already told you. I know that when this railcar moved - and it moved fast - I had never seen anything like this before. Later when we arrived at the end station I was feeling sick, and the other people that were there also felt the same way.

One of the guards said it happens the first time to everyone. When we came outside we were given goggles and asked to go through a security check. This is where it all gets weird. There were guards with weapons all over the place... and remember I told you about the energy fields that one has to go through. I was thinking I should not be here at this place, and I was a little scared. Then we got through this energy field and came to another room. I saw that there was a screen on the side of the wall that said HUMAN - NOT HUMAN - PURE - NOT PURE.

After I saw this I was thinking: Are there "NOT HUMANS" too?? At the energy field check-in there was a screen, which I mentioned before. There was a weird language on the screen. I have never seen this before. Underneath it stood letters that were like the "E" I told you about – but the only thing I could read was HUMAN - NOT HUMAN - PURE - NOT PURE.

The guards stopped us and told us to change clothes inside another room and come with them. When we had done so they said that it was time to go further down. Again, I was thinking how large is this place? We just came out of a rail system that runs for miles and miles... and then there is more?

We were then taken to a lift system, with seats, that was going to take us down... or, this is what I thought it was going to do. But it went sideways for about three minutes. In this place, time was not known to me because we had no way of telling what the time was. They had taken everything away from us at the check-ins.

At the lift I remember I saw a letter that look like a headphone – like the hearing phones you have on your head when listening to music. It was just bent like that if you see it from the front side and pointing down.

All I can say is that when our job was done I was thinking that the world is not as it seems to be, and that many things are hidden from the public. It makes me sad and scared.

Later, when I got into politics, I began digging into this because I needed more answers. What I found out was that these bases were Arks for the government and some of the people and military to survive inside. There was a threat from outside that was going to be in the year 2022 and that the human species had to survive.

The "Planet X" I learned about is from all what I have seen till now. The government knows this and is keeping it from the public. They have been tracking this object for a long time now and were given the first warnings from the USA. I know that 18 bases exist in Norway.

Out Of The Darkness – UFO Revelations And Planet X

I don't know what many of the dangers are because I am not a scientist. But what I know is that before 2022 the different governments are going to leave for the bases that they have built for the last 40 or 50 years. If this object goes by, there will be a lot of problems on the surface of the Earth. That is all I know. This is why they go underground. If such an event comes, they have made sure that five years or more underground is going to be what they need to avoid this. When they know it's safe to surface, they will rebuild again. We were just told that we have to leave before 2022 and that there is something in space that is going to cause much destruction.

I don't know if there is a threat from the sun itself. I am not so much into the science of things. I am just telling what I have seen and nothing more.

I can say that I have already said too much, but the people are now warned about this...

I have no need to make this up or create mass panic. I just want to tell the public what is to come, and I have done what I can from my side.

There are things in this world that are not known to the public. And there is one thing I can say about all this:

Be ready and have faith in yourself. There is no help in trusting the governments. Trust only yourself.

We should note that with the doom and gloom coming from the alleged Norwegian politician, there is some good news concerning 2022 as Tibetan monks expects friendly extraterrestrials to save mankind from whatever will happen to us that year.

Remote viewing is nothing new in Tibetan monasteries. For thousands of years remote viewing in the middle of other spiritual activities have dominated Tibetan culture. What some Indian tourists came to learn from a few Tibetan monasteries under the current Chinese rule is extremely alarming and fascinating.

According to these tourists remote viewers are seeing world powers in the course of self-destruction. They also see that the world will not be destroyed. Between now and 2022 the world super powers will continue to engage in regional wars. Terrorism and covert war will be the main problem. In world politics something will happen in and around 2020. At that time the world powers will threaten to destroy each other.

Out Of The Darkness – UFO Revelations And Planet X

In various cultures, planet Nibiru is known by many names, such as: Planet X, The Twelfth Planet, Marduk, Paradise, Nemisis, "Heaven" and the "Kingdom of the Heavens." Although Nibiru has been called The Twelfth Planet, technically it is not a planet of our solar system. In fact, it is a planet from another solar system and the star that was the sun of its solar system has been extinguished. Millions of years ago, the brown-dwarf star, along with the Planet Nibiru, was caught in the gravitational field of the sun, producing a binary star system. This uneasy alliance brought Nibiru into the solar system every 3600 years. The eccentric orbit of Nibiru gave the Anunnaki the advantage of having a mobile observatory from which they could observe and investigate many other planets near its orbit, especially planet Earth.

Out Of The Darkness – UFO Revelations And Planet X

Between 2020 and 2022, the whole world will get polarized and prepare for the ultimate doomsday. Heavy political maneuvers and negotiations will take place with little progress.

In 2022, the world will start plunging into a total destructive nuclear war. And at that time something remarkable will happen, says, Buddhist monk of Tibet. Supernatural divine powers will intervene. The destiny of the world is not to self-destruct at this time.

Scientific interpretation of the monks, statements makes it evident that the ET powers are watching us every step of the way. They will intervene in 2022 and save the world from self-destruction.

When asked about recent UFO sightings in India and China, the monks smiled and said the divine powers are watching us all. Mankind cannot and will not be allowed to alter the future to that great extent.

Monks also mentioned that beyond 2022 our current civilization would understand that the final frontier of science and technology is in area of spirituality and not material physics and chemistry. Beyond 2022, out technologies will take a different direction; people will learn the essence of spirituality, the relation between body and the soul, the reincarnation and the fact we are connected with each other are all part of God.

In India and China UFO sightings have increased in many folds. Many say the Chinese and Indian Governments are being contacted by the extraterrestrials. In recent days most UFO activities have been seen in those countries that have indigenously developed nuclear capabilities.

When asked if these extraterrestrials will show up in reality in 2022, the answers remote viewers are giving is: they will reveal themselves in such a way that none of us scared. They will reveal themselves only if they have to. As our science and technology progresses, we are destined to see them and interact with them any way.

According to the remote viewers, our Earth is blessed and is being saved continuously from all kinds of hazards all the time that we are not even aware of. As our technologies progress we will realize how external forces saved us.

CHAPTER TEN
The Fallen Angel Samyaza's Prophecy of Doom
By Poke Runyon

IN OUR RECENT science fiction film BEYOND LEMURIA Samyaza, leader of the Fallen Angels (an Annunaki or one of Richard Shaver's Norns), descends in a UFO to the summit of Mt. Shasta where he reveals the lost history of the human race and predicted our coming doom in the year 2012. Although this film is presented as "fiction," in the same way the Shaver Mystery was revealed seventy years ago, there is more behind it than mere entertainment.

Samyaza will be familiar to Biblical students as the chief of the rebellious angels in the ancient Ethiopian Book of Enoch. He appears as I originally channeled him in 1978 with horns, pointed ears and a third eye. He delivers his prophecy in the Enochian language—a spiritual tongue first translated into English by the 16th century wizards John Dee and Edward Kelley.

The following excerpt is taken directly from the BEYOND LEMURIA film script and the booklet accompanying the film entitled WISDOM OF THE AVATARS OF MT. SHASTA.

The giant figure of Samyaza looms over the summit of the mystic mountain and declares:

"I am Samyaza, first among those you call The Fallen Angels. We were the Elder Gods of your myths, the 'Elohim' of your scripture. We were the Titans and the Atlans, the founders of Lemuria and Atlantis, the "Giants in the Earth...

We advanced your intelligence. We evolved you to serve our needs. We taught you the rudiments of science – but not the refinements of philosophy...

We gave you knowledge but not wisdom.

When the world tottered on its axis, with the coming of the Dark Star, Many of us fled outward to distant worlds, while others descended under the earth, leaving you, our children, upon the surface to struggle upward from savagery to civilization only to fall back into barbarism with each cyclic return of the Cosmic Nemesis!

With the scientific advancements of your Third Age you might have saved your culture, but you seared the planet with atomic fire and sank into brutish ignorance even before the Dark Star returned to bring on the Great Flood.

Now, once again the Doom comes soon upon you. You have six of your years left to save your civilization. This living rock book and its Prophecy is our last gift to you. Read it carefully and heed it well."

Samyaza holds up a sliced geode disc – like the rock slices Richard Shaver used in his artwork – in his mechanical hands and recites in Enochian while we read the translation in English across the face of the disc:

"The Dark Star shall return time and time again, and shall bring the curse of storms, fire, earthquakes and darkness unto the Earth!

When the Monarch of the Heavens is veiled from view men must descend underground or die!"

Out Of The Darkness – UFO Revelations And Planet X

(Note: Samyaza was the leader of 200 rebel angels who descended to Earth according to The Book of Enoch. The prophecy predicts the cyclic return of Planet X according to the Mayan long count calendar.)

Readers who follow these subjects will find the above hauntingly familiar. The late Arthur C. Clarke predicted that when we finally came face-to-face with our creators we would be shocked to discover that they most resembled the devils we had feared! Using the Enochian angelic language and the Enochian Watchtower Tablets I had channeled Baraquel, Peneme, Azazel and Samyaza back in 1978. They appeared with horns, pointed ears and a third eye. They conveyed the mystery of the Mountain of Darkness as described in the Sepher ha Zohar.

In selecting an actor to portray Samyaza in our film I could make no better choice than Frater Solomon. He is the world famous psychic who predicted 9/11 and the War on Terror (see Dark Mirror of Magick DVD). Although Solomon delivers the prophecy in an inspired state of mind, I must take responsibility for its revelations – and frankly I now wish I had been less inspired.

In the same March-April issue of *NEXUS* Magazine, carrying our BEYOND LEMURIA ad on page ten, there was an article on the Norwegian government's extensive preparations to survive the coming encounter with Planet X. Massive excavations to create a labyrinth of underground bunkers were reported.

I had picked up the *NEXUS* issue at the Post Office that day just before dinner. By the time I had seen our ad and read the Planet X article it was time for the 6:30 evening news on television. There was Brian Williams on NBC transferring us to Ann Carey on location from a Norwegian island near the Arctic Circle. Carey came to us live from a huge underground bunker complex where the Norwegian government, in cooperation with other nations around the world, were preserving all of the plant seeds necessary to restore the Earth's vegetation following a planet-wide catastrophic event.

It is F.C.C. policy to treat such announcements "lightly" or even with derision, but in this case Ann Carey and especially Brian Williams were quite serious. Williams even seemed worried. The only touch of dry humor was Carey's mention of the local polar bears as an additional deterrent at this maximum-security installation.

Months before 9/11 we had sent Frater Solomon's Vassago Millennium Prophecy predicting the coming War on Terror (Dark Mirror of Magick DVD) off to the Copyright Office.

Poke Runyon At Teotihuacan, Mexico – 1988

Out Of The Darkness – UFO Revelations And Planet X

When we finally received the PA form it was stamped "September 11, 2001." Coincidences like this don't just happen by chance. Now I was seeing another such confirmation and, as before, I wished we hadn't been right.

At this point I should back up and do some explaining before going any further. Because there has been so much speculation and conjecture, along with disinformation and censorship both pro and con, regarding this Planet X phenomena we should make a few things clear before proceeding. First: there are several different interpretations of what "Planet X" is and the title has been applied to different hypothetical celestial objects. Rather than review the whole 200 year history of new planet hunting from Neptune to Chiron, and up to the most recent discovery of UB313 beyond Pluto in 2006, we should define what our particular Planet X is and is not.

There is an outer 'asteroid belt' beyond Neptune called the Kuiper belt. This flat ring of celestial debris – which includes Pluto, now demoted to a planetoid – is an extension of our Solar System. As such it lies on the plane of the ecliptic. Astronomers do continually discovering new asteroids and even planetoids (UB313 in 2006) inhabit the Kuiper belt – and each new discovery is called "Planet X." However, our massive, long-period cosmic nemesis, the dark planet Zecharia Sitchin calls "Nibiru," Richard Shaver referred to as "Nord," and Samyaza calls "the Dark Star" in our film, is a huge, dark, hot-core planet that has its origin in a vast, spherical region of space which completely surrounds our Solar System. Looking outward in any direction from our Sun, this sphere extends one to three light years in depth. It is called the "Oort Cloud" and is made up of countless thousands of comets. Some of these comets regularly orbit our Sun but, unlike planets and asteroids, their orbits are tangent to the ecliptic – in other words they can enter the Solar System from above or below our planetary plane. Comets with short period orbits are those which return in less than 200 years, whereas long period comets can take as long as 9,000 years to make a return visit.

But aren't comets just big, dirty snowballs? Unfortunately they are not. Comets have a solid nucleus with a hot core. The core is so hot that it discharges plasma through vents like so many volcanoes, hence the bright incandescence and the long, glowing tail. As an example astro-physicist James M. McCanney cites the comet Hale-Bopp as having a huge, solid core almost as large as our moon! The damage Shoemaker-Levy 9 created when it impacted Jupiter was far beyond what a "dirty snowball" could affect.

Now our particular "Planet X" is so big that its hot core is largely contained. It may have a few active volcanoes like Earth does, but not enough to be seen by the Hubble telescope even if we knew where to look. It is effectively a big, dark 'stealth planet.' We know it exists by the evidence of its previous visits, both here on Earth and out in the Solar System. Our history, our geological record and our mythology – including the calculations of the Mayan long-count calendar – tend to establish its long-period orbit at about 5,000 years.

Samyaza warns us: "When the Monarch of the Heavens (Jupiter) is veiled from view (eclipsed by the Dark Star) men must descend underground or die!"

We should recall (and the Draconians have not forgotten) that 65 million years ago the Earth was impacted by a large asteroid that wiped out the dinosaurs. The small burrowing mammals survived only because they lived underground. We are their descendents – and according to legend and recent scientific discoveries in human genome development, visitors from that same Dark Star may have transformed us from primates to Homo sapiens.

I first learned about the Dark Star from my mentor in archaeology Professor *******, a curator at the Los Angeles Museum of Natural History. In 1975 he was leading a paleontology survey expedition in Baja California sponsored by the National Geographic Society. I was then a graduate student in anthropology at Cal State, Northridge and a member of the expedition. In the evenings around the campfire the professor mentioned his theory of a recurring catastrophic celestial event based on his knowledge of ancient Mayan and Aztec cyclic calendar calculations.

In 1988 the professor had become a department head at the University of Mexico. By that time I had received my master's degree in anthropology and had just returned from my own expedition to the ruined city of Nan Modal out in the Central Pacific (see Beyond Lemuria). Prof. ******* invited me down to Mexico to take part in a UNAM expedition. We surveyed the earliest know Olmec pictographs deep in a cavern down in Gurrero and even discovered a buried pyramid that had not been penetrated by treasure hunters. Once again the subject of conversation turned to the Dark Star. Dr. ******* was even more convinced that his theory was correct. When we returned from the field he told me there was something that I should see at the Anthropological Museum in Mexico City.

It was October 31; the Day of the Dead. Before we visited the Museum we drove out to **Teotihuacan** to make our traditional climb to the top of the Pyramid of the Sun. The steps were so steep that my otherwise strong legs were soon aching. The professor explained that this was engineered on purpose to exhaust the sacrificial victim before the priests at the top ripped his heart from his body.

The top was a square platform affording a magnificent view of the surrounding ruins. There was a small crowd already there; mostly tourists but off to one side I noticed a huddle of Mexican college students with their backs turned toward the rest of us. They were trying to conceal something...and then suddenly they raised open mason jars over their heads and released a squadron of monarch butterflies.

The souls of dead.

I recalled D. H. Lawrence's novel *The Feathered Serpent*. Paganism was still alive in Mexico!

And then we went to the Museum in downtown Mexico City. The main gallery is dedicated to Mexica (Aztec) exhibits. Foremost among these is the huge Sun Stone which has been called "the Aztec Calendar" but what my professor wanted me to see was something else – something I will never forget.

Standing on a black pedestal and looming up over our heads was the most utterly evil image I have ever beheld! It was a hideous combination of snakes, skulls and claws that combined to form a giant monster radiating a malignant power one scarcely encounters outside of a nightmare. It was Coatlicue, mother of the mysterious "400 from the South" and the blue-skinned warrior god Huitzilopochtli, patron deity of the Aztec Empire.

"This is the most frightening thing I've ever seen," I commented.

"They loved her," the professor said.

"Goddess of the Apocalypse?" I asked.

"Goddess of Earth and death," he replied. "You'll notice that her head is missing."

In a flash I saw it in my mind's eye: It was an Aztec stylization of an antediluvian being. Was this Dark Mother, with her necklace of hands and hearts so similar to Kali and Anath, something from the bowels of the Earth or from the Dark Star?

Zacharia Sitchin believes that the deep-space dark planet Nibiru is still inhabited; if so then there are certain conditions and factors we must assume. In order to maintain a civilized society on a dark planet in deep space (we should say in a dark planet, not on it) a highly advanced technology would be required. The thermal and electromagnetic energy of the planet itself would have to be extensively controlled and exploited. This would mean no earthquakes, volcanic eruptions or impacts from other celestial bodies would be permitted. The whole hard crust of the planet would be a honeycomb of super-solidified subterranean chambers. All food would be grown underground or synthesized. Air generation and circulation for such a complex would be far beyond our level of technology. Water would have to be conserved and recycled with efficiency we can hardly imagine.

What we are describing is what Carl Sagan and Michio Kaku would call a Class 1.5 Civilization whereas our present level is about 0.7. These beings would classify us on a level of stone-age primitives at best and chimpanzees at worst. They would probably have achieved inter-dimensional mobility. The research of French scientist Jacques Vallee strongly indicates this capability. According to Vallee the genuine close encounters on record are probably inter-dimensional – and most are probably not extra terrestrial.

These Dark Star people may have been our original creators and some of their progeny may secretly survive here on Earth in another extra-dimensional subterranean world as close as the mirror in our bathroom, and as far away as the dark side of the moon. Apparently some of the super-human beings under our Earth and beyond our Solar System are friendly to us –while their sub-human counterparts, the Deros, have been our secret enemies since prehistoric times.

We explore these possibilities in our film Beyond Lemuria.

Poke Runyon
Writer-Producer: Beyond Lemuria

Out Of The Darkness – UFO Revelations And Planet X

POLAR SHIFT AND THE DROWNING OF AMERICA
By Timothy Green Beckley

RECENTLY 49 of the 50 states underwent a deep freeze – part of a Polar Vortex. Ice dripped from power lines and trees and temperatures went down well below zero in places where 40 degrees in January would not be unusual.

There is, as most well know, a great debate over whether the planet is undergoing a global warming. It has become a hot button topic with political polarization a giant part of the issue. If nothing else, no one can dispute that our globe is in the middle of a change in climate.

One of the effects of Planet X being in our solar system – hidden or not – would be a drastic pull on our planet's axis resulting in a shifting of the poles. The end result of which would be dramatic melting of the ice caps and tidal waves up and down the East and West coasts.

THE ULTIMATE DISASTER AND THE AWAKENING

The ultimate disaster say many seers, may be a polar shift in which our entire planet would flip end over end in space. The result would be upheaval the likes of which we can only imagine. If the earth were to slip from its current axis, the polar ice caps could end up in the tropical zone, and our warm climates would turn suddenly cold.

Ruth Montgomery, Edgar Cayce, Paul Solomon, Nostradamus, Helena Blavatsky and the Hopi Indians all predict that the Earth will flip on its axis. Most envision this as happening shortly – usually around the year 2020.

Writer and researcher Dorothy Starr of San Diego has become a spokesperson on the subject. This is how she outlines the potentially catastrophic situation. "The Antarctic Ice Cap is enormous. It would cover the United States and most of Canada. Ice is two miles high at the Pole. Unless the growth is controlled it will tip over the earth causing a world flood.

Hugh Auchincloss Brown, an engineer explains in *CATACLYSMS OF THE EARTH* how this will be done.

"The earth, says the Engineer, is stabilized and held to its Axis of (North, South Poles) by the centrifugal force of the equatorial bulge. The gyroscopic energy of the rotating bulge steadies the globe and keeps it from rolling haphazardly.

"The earth thus functions in the manner of a flywheel."

"The wobble of the earth results in a wandering of the Pole of Figure, the center of gyration of the polar ice caps. The linear speed of the ice caps increases at about 6.28 times their distance from the Axis of Spin; the total energy of motion and the 'throw' of centrifugal force of the ice caps both increase proportionally with the weight of the ice mass that is off-center and at a rate which is the square of its velocity. The speed of travel is a function both of rotation and the wobble of the earth. As the ice cap grows the wobble of the earth gives it a greater and greater linear motion which shows in an increased centrifugal force, and this tends to provide greater inertia until the stabilizing effect of the earth bulge is overcome and the earth rolls sideways to its direction of rotation. This flings the poles toward the equator and equator lands toward the poles.

"Rhinoceroses have been found in the permanently frozen ground of the Arctic regions, showing that tropical lands were flung pole-ward. Mammoths are found in upright position with grass in their mouths and stomachs. They were suddenly killed by the tipping earth rushing their grazing lands to the Arctic. Some have broken bones as if the terrible winds of the tip-over had tossed them about then buried them under the debris where they quickly froze in their new cold climate. There they remained thousands of years to tell us today the story of the earth's tipping.

"Great loads of bones of horses, cattle, camels and other animals were found in the frozen tundra of Siberia. How did they get there if the earth did not roll their grazing lands pole-ward. Surely the frozen tundra could not supply vegetation to feed such hordes. "Mr. Brown gives us much more evidence from fossils, sea life, legends and archaeology of the former tip-overs or 'careens' of the earth.

"There is palemagnetic evidence. Rocks show the periodic reversal of earth's geomagnetic field. See DEBATE ABOUT THE EARTH (Hitoshi Takeuchi, Seiya Uyeda and Hiroo Kanamori) pp. 149-51. Also the U.S. Geological Survey Report in SCIENCE 144, 1964 pp. 1537-43, titled, Reversals of the Earth's Magnetic Field, (R.R. Doell, A. Cox). From these magnetic reversals north was once south, it seems. Well, the old poles DO get around! For years Mr. Brown has said the poles have moved over the earth; now we find the rocks agree with him.

IS THE ICE CAP REALLY GROWING?

"THE POLAR ICE CAPS (A. Bauer, C. Lorius) 1964 says the, volume of ice IS increasing annually enough to lower the sea level and that the sea level increase may be due to the expansion of water as a result of higher ocean temperatures. THE DYNAMICS OF THE ANTARCTIC ICE COVER (Markov, K.K.) 1962, says the Antarctic Ice Sheet has grown. Dr. P.A. Shumsky reported at the Symposium in Helsinki, 1960, that the South Polar Ice Cap grows at the rate of 293 cubic miles of ice a year. (See Mr. Brown's News Release.) Dr. Malcolm Mellors of Australia corroborated the Cap's growth. "Not all glaciologists agree on the Cap's growth, but if just one has evidence of growth that should cause investigation."

Likewise, John White, a Cheshire, Connecticut resident, and a veteran researcher in the fields of parascience and consciousness awakening, has spent the past several years collecting a wealth of material pertaining to this great pole shift. A former research associate of astronaut Edgar Mitchell, the articulate magazine and book author believes that there is a good possibility the earth rotated at least once before, and is likely to do so once again sometime before the year 2020.

In order to get to the bottom of the matter, White has spent considerable time checking out the predictions of both select scientists and New Age seers who maintain that Terra Firma is in for a mighty jolt in the not so distant future.

"There are three main groups that independently predict a pole shift in this century," states White. "The first are the ancient prophecies spoken of in the Bible and by such soothsayers as Nostradamus. Edgar Cayce and Rev. Paul Solomon who maintained that on May 5, 2000, there will be a grand alignment of the planets which will induce shifting of the earth's crust. There is also Aaron Abrahams, a psychic in Washington State who said that in the year 1999 or 2000 the Earth will tumble on its axis a full 180 degrees, but the core of the earth will tumble only about 90 degrees so that the poles will in effect be projecting through the Equatorial regions. At this moment the present ice caps will build up in the polar locations. In addition to the ancient prophecies and the contemporary psychics, there are modern scientifically-oriented researchers who. also claim that there is a pole shift coming."

Among the scientists White refers to are Hugh Auchincloss Brown, an electrical engineer who before his death at the age of 96, devoted more than 60 years of his life to the promulgation of his theory that a vast polar ice cap would tip the earth over toward the end of this century and wipe out civilization. Also, quoted by White in his book "**Poleshift**" (published by Doubleday) are the likes of Chan Thomas, a West Coast-based cosmologist, Charles Hapgood, a friend of Albert Einstein, and Adam Barber, an independent investigator who started his own foundation for advocates of the polar shift theory.

At a symposium which I organized in New York City, John White revealed the fact that his research has fully determined that a number of UFO contactees and channels have also been predicting a polar shift, as sort of a climax to earth changes that are getting under way now and will be continuing right on through to the end of this century.

What I find so fascinating about John White's work is that he looks at the potential outcome of a global disaster in a much different way than you might expect. He tries to see things in a positive light and says that we do have a chance to survive - that if we are destroyed we will have no one to blame but ourselves.

"Many of the predictions say that it will be the human factor - we ourselves - that will be of critical importance in either triggering or preventing these earth changes. In essence, the psychics say that the state of our consciousness will determine the outcome of the approaching crisis."

John credits anthropologist and archaeologist, Dr. Jeffrey Goodman with devising a term to cover this human factor which will prove most important in determining our future state of affairs.

"In the book *'We Are the Earthquake Generation*,' Dr. Goodman uses the word 'Bio-relativity' to describe how human beings are effecting through the power of their thoughts everything that exists around them. Consciously or unconsciously our behavior has an influence on the totality of the earth. In this regard the prophecies tell us that virtuous living and respect for the earth can have a stabilizing impact. Prayer is a familiar form of this influence, but better yet would be the development of a steadily focused consciousness amongst the people that would recognize the mutual dependence of the human race and the cosmos, and the interdependence that we have on each other that really makes us the co-creators of our destiny."

John suggests that such a state of consciousness operating among the human race would have a strong, positive bearing on the future trials and tribulations.

"The native Americans say we should 'walk in balance on the Earth Mother,' and if we don't the alternative is simple. If we continue our disregard for the sacredness of life, if we continue our crimes against nature and our fellow humans, the outcome could be beak.

AN IMPORTANT CONVERSATION WITH JOHN WHITE

Around the time that his book **POLESHIFT** was published, I sat down with John and quizzed him extensively on a possible tilting of the Earth. This subject is certain to be of grave relevance to all of us.

Here are some excerpts from our conversation:

Beckley: Looking to the future, if there were a polar shift in our lifetime, would that wipe out most of civilization?

White: My book *Poleshift* deals principally with the predictions and prophecies of another pole shift, a future one which is to occur by the end of this century - 1999 to 2000. A number of groups have independently predicted this. There are various ancient prophecies, notably those of the Bible, and the oracle Nostradamus, who say that the earth is probably going to tumble on its axis or shift its crust. They're not specific about the way this is going to happen.

Beckley: Specifically, what does the Bible say?

White: In Revelation it says that the earth will undergo an earth- quake greater than has ever been recorded before, and by extension - since we do know that earthquakes do jolt the axis of the earth - this could produce a very traumatic pole shift.

Beckley: Is there evidence leading up to this?

White: In addition to the prophecies and the contemporary psychics, there are modern scientifically-oriented researchers who also claim that there is a pole shift coming. Immanuel Velakovsky, by the way did not predict another one. He simply dealt with the evidence of the previous ones. Another researcher is Professor Charles Hapgood who wrote a book called **THE PATH OF THE POLES**. Actually that was the title of the revised edition. The first edition was called **EARTH'S SHIFTING CRUST**. The introduction to that book was actually written by Albert Einstein, who endorsed Hapgood's notion. Of those who say another one is likely, nearly all of them agree that a pole shift will occur at the end of this century. But not all of them say that it is inevitable.

Out Of The Darkness – UFO Revelations And Planet X

Beckley: Why did they say that it would happen at the end of the 20th century?

White: That's a good question. I'm not really able to answer except to the extent that a number of factors have been identified by the various predictions and prophecies as being the trigger mechanisms or contributing some degree of influence to a forthcoming pole shift. These various factors - which are both internal to the earth and external, and natural as well as man- made - are acting at different rates of speed and with different rates of influence. However, they are all converging at whatever their speed might be so as to come together at the end of this century, or thereabouts.

Beckley: You're talking now about the increase in earthquakes, volcanic eruptions, and so forth?

White: We are seeing evidence right now that the prophecies are being fulfilled. Clearly, the earth is coming out of a period in which it has been relatively free from earthquakes and volcanic activity, and is entering a time when seismic activity is stepping up. We are seeing more earthquakes, and more powerful earthquakes every year. We're seeing long-dormant volcanoes starting to erupt. There is one in Japan that erupted in October of 1979, and it has never been known in all of history to have erupted before.

This is a hotly debated topic, and by and large the scientific community does not accept it. But, I should say that on the other side of the question there is an informal study done by a friend of mine in Connecticut, who looked at the data available on four different volcanoes, two in the Caribbean and two in Italy. What he did was to plot the frequency of eruption for these volcanoes over the 1st 200 to 300 years. He found that these volcanoes, all four of them' are erupting more and more frequently. When he plotted out the eruption patterns for each of them, he discovered that all four converged in a 1982-1984 time period.

You asked what the effect of a pole shift would be. Within 24 hours, the results would be this: First of all the oceans would spill out of their basins and just overrun the land masses, in massive tidal waves. There would be huge earthquakes greater than we've ever measured. Volcanoes would erupt around the world. Poisonous gases and ash would fill the atmosphere. The earth itself would be tumbling through space at speeds of hundreds of miles an hour so in effect, anything living on the surface of the earth would experience hurricane winds of several hundred miles an hour. The face of the globe would change instantly. Not only climates, climatic zones, but land masses would rise and fall. Geography itself would change, and of course living organisms, including people, would. be eliminated. There would be unprecedented destruction and death. Some predictions say that 90 percent or more of people on the earth would be killed in such a pole shift.

Beckley: Would we have any kind of luck in preventing such a global disaster?

White: This is a good example of how we can directly affect those predictions and prophecies. We can also do it through parapsychological means as well as overt behavior. We have seen recently the emergence of PK ability, or psychokinesis, especially in young children around the world. Hundreds of youngsters are developing the ability to bend metal and influence matter using the power of their minds. Let's imagine that this trait emerges very quickly in the human race on a global scale. Conceivably if it were developed to a sufficient degree, in a large number of people, through the direct influence of mind over matter, we could pacify – we could stabilize – the earth even though it would be on the point of a pole shift. This is sort of science fantasy, but it's not totally incredible or beyond imagination.

Beckley: Granted, but would we have enough warning to so something like this?

White: The warning is in the predictions and prophecies. We have at most 20 years according to these predictions and prophecies. Now, I'm not saying this is going to happen. I'm saying that there is a serious case for a pole shift happening, and that the scientific community especially should examine it.

Beckley: Are you at all familiar with the fact that in UFO literature, the various UFO contactees who say they are having physical contact or telepathic contact with extraterrestrial beings are being told pretty much the same thing?

White: Yes, I am. In fact, I have a chapter in my book which covers one such prediction. It was made through Biard Wallace in Grosskill, Michigan, d the alleged communicants are the Space Brothers. The Space Brothers told Biard Wallace and his group that the whole solar system is moving into a new sector of space where the vibratory quality is going to be such as to change consciousness in the human race. At the same time, a new star will come into the solar system which will shift the center of gravity from its present location to another one as the solar system becomes a binary star solar system. The shift of the center of gravity will affect all the planets. Some will leave their orbits. Others will just get a shaking up in their orbits. But conceivably a pole shift could be devastating not only on earth but on other planets. And according to the Space Brothers, this will take place within the next 15 years.

Beckley: Are they going to try to do something to prevent this from happening?

White: I've not heard anything, or read anything in any communications about this. What they're trying to do, essentially, is awaken the human race to the possibility and encourage us to develop our own powers and abilities.

Beckley: Are they offering advice in this regard. Do you see this as an overall pattern in all of the experiences?

White: There is a pattern of sorts. By no means is there agreement from all the communications, from extraterrestrials and ultraterrestrials. But generally speaking, the thrust of the communications is that a time of change is coming upon the earth.

On a positive note, John concludes by noting that there is a way out of the situation we are in. "The predictions and prophecies all say that if we don't mend our ways we will have created a situation in which the planet is destabilized. The pole shift will result in destroying most life on our planet.

"To a man, all of those we have sought knowledge from fully agree that even though these devastating events may occur, after the earth has settled down, a Golden Age will flourish for the first time since the days of Adam and Eve."

"The earth changes," states John White, "will never-the-less open up a niche in the environment for new life forms to emerge. The human race will be cleansed from the Earth Mother because it has become an irritating, infectious disease. But note that it will not be a case of our being punished for our sins. From the prospective of Bio-relativity it will be a case of being punished by our sins. It's instant Karma – getting back what we give. According to the prophecies there will be some survivors. These survivors will be the seedbed for a new race – a higher humanity – which will evolve in an accelerated fashion. The new race will know from first hand experiences what the terrible consequences are for failing to walk in balance upon the Earth Mother. The new race will know how to live in harmony with the cosmos and they will inherit the earth."

D-DAY SEERS SPEAK

To sum up and review these amazing psychic and UFO revelations, we call upon New Age teacher and master alchemist Michael X. Barton, author of many titillating monographs, to review the subject in the form of a series of questions which he asked of those who have firsthand knowledge of the situation which is based on first hand visionary experiences.

Question: "Can you give me a clear word picture of D-DAY?"

Answer: "Yes. There are astrological signs foretelling that the Great Polar Shift will come soon. There will be great cataclys.ms, and geological changes. The atomic blasts in the west have intensely aggravated the San Andreas Fault. It will crack wide open soon and great tremors will shake the state of California . . .and it will gradually submerge.

"At the time of the Shift there will be a terrific chain of earth- quakes. Japan, two-thirds of the British Isles and the countries of the warring nations of Europe and the Balkans will be submerged. The Suez Canal will become an open waterway, due to the submergence of the land thereabout.

"New York City will be hit by a terrific earthquake and be sub- merged. Mountainous tidal waves will engulf the Atlantic coast- line hundreds of miles inland. We will have a 50-foot flood level in Pittsburgh. Washington, D.C. will be flooded. The submerged is- lands of Atlantis will rise up in the Atlantic.

"A huge continent will rise up in the Pacific. The New Jerusalem will descend upon it. In the New Age (after the Great Polar Shift) you will be able to travel by water from the Gulf of Mexico to Hudson Bay; from Denver to Moscow. The Great Shift will come at the time of atomic warfare, which will be of short duration." -Brother Joseph A. Lageman, Pittsburgh, PA.

Out Of The Darkness – UFO Revelations And Planet X

Question: "What places may be considered 'safety areas'?"

Answer: "We agree with the Mormons that the Rocky Mountain area is the best place in the world; that is, the area between the Sierra Nevada and Rocky Mountains. That takes in most of Colorado, the western part, the whole of Utah, most of Idaho and the northern part of Arizona. Montana and Wyoming should be good, for they have all the necessary factors for safety.

"That gives you plenty of scope. That doesn't mean to say that these are the only safe places. We believe the western part of Pennsylvania should be good, providing you are far enough away from the industrial cities, and have a good elevation. The minimum should be 2,000 feet. 4,000 would be better. And don't forget that the range of the atom bomb is much greater today than it was when tried in Japan.

"Keep away from large bodies of water, either oceans or lakes.., Many lakes will spill their contents when the earth CHANGES ITS AXIS, which it is going to do. As far as the enemy is concerned, we believe certain cities will be immune from sabotage and warfare. But that does not exclude them from danger from the elements, such as earthquakes, cyclones, tornadoes, and tidal waves. And so, as the good Lord cleanses the earth, we must get out into the wide open spaces, and live close to nature. We shall be stripped of things that come from our artificial civilization, things that we do not need anyway. Not only will the land be cleansed, but HUMANITY WILL BE PURGED.

"Let me emphasize that all COASTAL REG IONS are dangerous, for there will be tidal waves such as have never prevailed in modern times, due to the sinking of large bodies of land and the rising of others. It is more likely that the islands of Japan will sink into the Pacific; and that close to the American coast will be. the rising of a huge body of land, a portion if not the whole of ancient Lemuria. Tidal waves on the East Coast are apt to reach a height of from 1,000 to 2,000 feet. And so from that, you can see that the coastal regions are all dangerous." - Excerpt from "**THE COMING STORM**" by William Kullgren, Atascadero, California.

Question: "Is D-DAY inevitable, or can it be prevented?"

Answer: "No predicted event is entirely inevitable. Reverse forces, used in the present moment, can always minimize, lessen or prevent a future event from happening in the way it is likely to. According to Hugh

Out Of The Darkness – UFO Revelations And Planet X

Auchincloss Brown, E.E., we can postpone the impending flood. The suggested method is cutting many channels in the parapet of coastal rocks that form the basin which holds up the great ice reservoir (at South Pole). This will prevent the central glacial ice to drain off into the oceans by gravity. We have a rendezvous with Fate. We will become our own corporeal saviors by taking control of and limiting the further growth of the South Polar Ice Cap, or most of our race will perish in the flood."

Question: "What will precede the Great Polar Shift?"

Answer: "Maybe a war. Economic result: poverty, then starvation. Be ready for great changes in the twinkling of an eye. Prepare for SEVEN YEARS of struggle with the elements." - Oxtle of Mars. Received by L. D. of Oxnard, Calif., 5-18-59.

Question: "Who shall be taken up by the Space People on D- DAY?"

Answer: "As your Holy Prophesy so states, we shall save the elect. We stand by with our craft of all types and sizes. We are constantly prepared to land if and when it should become necessary to evacuate the elect to new homes on nearby planets where they will be our guests until your planet has been completely washed and cleansed and made fit once more to dwell upon . . . " Telethot communication received from Ashtar Command, Space Station Schare, by Carl A. Anderson, of Fullerton, California.

"Thousands will be rescued from off the land surfaces just prior to the cataclysmic upheavals. They will be levitated or lifted up, and taken aboard the craft you have chosen to call 'Flying Saucers' . . . There will be many who will not be taken up, who will be spared however. They will be in places of comparative safety when disaster strikes. They will be saved by the protective force-field emanating from the aura that surrounds their bodies . . . " -Message received by Automatic Writing by Carl A. Anderson on February 25, 1957, from a Master now in Tibet.

Question: "Shall we build boats or rafts for survival?"

Answer: "The masses will need them. Those whose aura radiates much light, with an abundance of the violet or purple tone will not need them. They shall be taken up. Your greatest protection lies in building your aura - filling it with more and more LIGHT - and cleansing it, day by day. The best way to expand and strength- en your aura with the light will be revealed to you very soon. Be alert to accept and apply this vital new information." -Lon-Zara received by Michael X.

"On August 26, 1958, a dear friend of mine, Wanda Brown and one of her friends, of Inglewood, California, were advised by Blaru (a being from another solar system) that the best kind of boat to build was 'circular and covered with a hatch. Food supplies sufficient for several months at sea should be taken.' I agree that the 'saucer-shaped' boat or raft is far superior to the ordinary kind. However, we are now being requested by our nearest planetary guardians to concentrate on building our spiritual aura rather than on building of the rafts." - Michael X.

Question: "What is happening to our Solar System now?"

Answer: "Several years ago our Solar System passed into a new phase called the '4thDensity'. This new phase is now changing our entire earth and our way of life. Prior to this time everything as we know it consisted of three Densities: Life, Motion, and Consciousness. Now a new and higher level of Life is going to occur. (The Spiritual or Christ Consciousness.) Every individual person whose (soul) education has been complete must PREPARE for this, this next step of our eternal existence. Those not ready must take this step over again. Our planet, entering this new Density, shall endure changes that will eventually be CATACLYSMIC in action.

"After the readjustment of our planet, a new way of life will begin. The people will enjoy the pleasure of space travel; there will be no disease nor sickness, hence no need for doctors or for hospitals. Everyone will communicate with each other through thought transference; the need for speech will not be. Wars, hatred and lust for power will be unheard of. Everyone will be on equal level. The Way of Life will be as the Creator intended it to be. Love, Peace and Harmony will reign supreme." -Telethot received by Russell Dunham of Fullerton, Calif.

Question: "What is my responsibility in these turbulent times?"

Answer: "New adventures, new lands, new friends – seek ye out those who are in accord. Be in rapport with those who are bearers of LIGHT. Seek ye the Ambassadors from out the Cosmic Realms. Many are the Ambassadors now come to GUIDE the race of man into pathways of light, lest man fall into the pit of destruction. Be thou aware of these Beings who are ever watchful of thy purpose.

"Open thy consciousness to their messages. Listen intently for their instruction. Ask that these shall be aware of thy cosmic contact DURING THE HOURS OF SLEEP. Pray thou will be cognizant of thy nightly experiences.

"Receptivity is for thy experience. Calm thyself and listen for the 'wee small voice'. Amplify this voice with thy enthusiasm and broad- cast it to the four corners of the Earth. BE THY VOICE !" - Larry Dodge of Oxnard, Calif. Telethot 8-22-56.

Michael concludes his findings with these closing words. "Again, dear friend, the Wise Ones of both ancient and modern times have spoken to us. They have spoken of D-DAY and what it will mean to you and me. Their words only serve to bring us closer in the bond of universal LOVE and UNDERSTANDING that exists between every living thing.

"It is important that you may share your love and light with others, wisely, but with NEW ZEAL For you – a NEW AGE Individual – have heard the CLARION CALL OF THE SEERS. And you have a place, a service, an opportunity to help bring in the glorious Millennium and GOD'S KINGDOM ON EARTH!"

Barbara Hudson, a UFO channeler, said that in a vision she saw New York being hit by a gigantic tidal wave, "In one vision, I saw myself inside Riverside Church somewhere high up - like in a tower. The only furnishings in the room I was in were a huge cross, a desk and a chair."

Through a nearby archway window, Barbara described to me how water seemed to be rising in every direction, covering most of the buildings in the vicinity.

"Suddenly, the floor I was standing on gave way, and I was positioned on a ledge looking down several hundred feet into the body of the Church."

Here, too, the water was rising, and it seemed that the dark green liquid would reach her in a matter of moments. At this point the vision faded. On another occasion, while giving medical treatment to a patient in St. Luke's Hospital, at Amsterdam Avenue and 114th Street, where she was an orderly, Barbara described how she had chanced to glance out the hospital window, since the room seemed to be obstructed by a strange color coming from somewhere outside.

"I noticed that the sun looked funny – almost orange-yellow

in color – with a strange fog that seemed to hover above the skyline. I then heard a rumble and saw water rolling over the city in every direction. Instead of one large tidal wave, the sky looked like an ocean of white-capped waves."

Between nearby Morningside Park and St. Luke's Hospital, Barbara explained, the street split, leaving a wide valley where seconds before hundreds of cars had been moving on it.

"At that, I looked back toward my patient for a brief moment and when I turned back the scene below was once again normal." Barbara Hudson's most frightening experience, however, happened even more recently. She walked over to the kitchen window near where I was seated and looked out through the storm screen.

"I was standing by this window and noticed that the sky and sun looked as it had done previously during my visions. I then saw what appeared to be a long grey line above the buildings, which seemed to be moving toward my apartment building."

Initially, Barbara thought this grey line was a strange formation of clouds.

"Then I noticed that the air was full of a deafening roar and the buildings were snapping in two as the 'cloud' passed over. As the grey line approached uptown I could see that this line was in reality a huge tidal wave."

It hit Riverside Church, Barbara told me as I listened attentively to her story. The force of the impact was so great that the entire foundation crumbled to the ground.

"Seeing this, I grabbed my young daughter by the arm," realizing the tidal wave would soon reach them, "and ran into the hall in an attempt to get to the roof. As I reached the stairway, I noticed that water had already began to pour in through the skylight and was filling up the stairwell and would reach our position soon.

"I noticed also that the water was seeping under the closed roof door. Frightened I might be swept down the stairs by the force of the raging tide, opened the door only a crack at first. Seeing that it was only a few inches deep, I pulled the door completely open and carried my daughter to the roof."

Once there, Barbara proceeded to climb onto a vent-type structure which rose an additional three or four feet from the rooftop. But even here the deadly water continued to rise. She stood at the kitchen window, only a few feet away from me, and continued with her frightening vision.

"Looking out over the city, I could see an identical situation, with only a few of the really tall buildings left uncovered. For those structures which had not been crushed by the force of the tidal wave itself were now completely covered by the still rising water."

When Barbara came out of her altered state the first thing she remembered is how vivid the vision had been.

"I remember saying, when I came around, 'Oh, my God, wish that this would never happen,' but I know it will, sometime in my lifetime."

Drawing by Barbara Hudson

THE END TIME VISIONS OF ANTHONY AND LYNN VOLPE

I was first introduced to Anthony and Lynn Volpe in Pittsburgh, Pennsylvania, where I had organized an all day conference on the UFO enigma. During a break in the proceedings they came forward to tell me they believed in UFOs and had actually made contact with amphibian beings from the constellation of Pegasus.

The Ivyland, Pennsylvania couple say that they have put together musical vibrations and recorded it on cassette tape and actually brought in a UFO during 1977, much like the scientists in *Close Encounters of the Third Kind* attempted to do.

"This music appears to have magical qualities about it," the heads of a local UFO group maintain, adding, that if they get permission from "our space friends," they may play the tape at a future seminar of mine and attempt to bring in a UFO, "or some sort of manifestation."

Regarding End Time prophecies the Volpe's say that the east coast will be flooded out before too many years have passed. Here is Lynn's account of her various experiences: "For the past seven years I have had visionary dreams of the flooding out of the eastern seaboard. The Atlantic Ocean would be seen moving in over the coastal areas rapidly and steadily. In my vision my house was uprooted and in astral travel, I was able to look down over the east coast, and it looked like the middle of the Atlantic. This flooding out will take place over a two year period and will also include the Midwestern section of the country, almost as far as the Mississippi River, Illinois and Indiana.

"In one vision I saw many small fissures in the earth, opening up along the east coast, pulling apart the land and causing water to erupt from these openings. These are 'mini fault lines' of which scientists know nothing.

"Another time, Trenton, New Jersey was being flooded out. People in the city were going up to the top of high rise buildings. There was a book there where people were checking to see if their name had been entered. This was called 'Mary's Book of Records.'

"These tidal waves and small cracks were being aggravated by constant atomic explosions. This 'baptism' of the east coast will be like a cleansing and redemption of the earth which will help people toward a greater awakening of universal brotherhood."

The visions of the Volpe's are quite stimulating to our mind, as they confirm what we have learned from other sources. Anthony recently found himself on board a space ship looking down at the earth as great changes were taking place.

"It was as if I belonged there, as sort of a 'dual existence' (author's note: Is this another possible example of 'Blends' or 'Star People' experiencing End Time events?). I looked down through a viewing port which was like a window in the floor and saw the earth, which appeared as large as a grapefruit at arm's length. It was my task to record what I was about to see, as I knew something important was to transpire at that moment; namely, changes within the earth's structure. Suddenly, the earth expanded as if it were a balloon being filled with air. It expanded about twenty per cent and then returned to its normal size. While in the expanded state, the topographical features were all disturbed. However, when the earth 'regrouped itself' or returned to its normal size, the surface was once again normal. As all this was taking place, I was busy recording the events from on board the space craft."

Out Of The Darkness – UFO Revelations And Planet X

COATLICUE, GODDESS OF EARTH AND DEATH

If you enjoyed this book, write for our free catalog of amazing books and mystifying DVDs:

Global Communications
P.O. Box 753
New Brunswick, NJ   08903

E-mail: mrufo8@hotmail.com

Visit our website:
www.conspiracyjournal.com

THE SECRET LOST DIARY OF ADMIRAL RICHARD E. BYRD AND THE PHANTOM OF THE POLES

EXPLORE A STRANGE LAND KEPT HIDDEN FROM THE PUBLIC. HERE FOR THE FIRST TIME IS THE SECRET DIARY OF ONE OF THE GREATEST ADVENTURERS WHO HAS EVER LIVED. PLUS PROOF THAT THERE IS A VAST, UNCHARTED, CIVILIZATION EXISTING INSIDE THE PLANET!

TWO BOOKS IN ONE! In addition to the text of Admiral Byrd's diary is a rare, "long lost" manuscript by William Reed who puts forward his theory that we live on the outside of a hollow globe. Based upon the journals of various seafarers who have explored the regions around the poles, Reed puts forward the following questions: 1. Why is the earth flattened at the poles? 2. Why have the poles never been reached? 3. Why does the sun not appear for so long in winter near the supposed poles? 4. Assuming that the earth is hollow, the interior should be warmer. 5. We must now resort to the compass. Does it refuse to work when drawing near the supposed poles? 6. Meteors are constantly falling near the supposed poles. Why? 7. The next query is concerning the great quantities of dust constantly found in the Arctic Ocean. What causes this dust? 8. What produces the Aurora Borealis? 9. Icebergs are next in order. Where are they formed? And how?? 10. What causes tidal waves? 11. What causes colored snow in the Arctic region? 12. Why are the nights so long in the polar regions? 13. What causes the great ice-pressure in the Arctic Ocean during still tide and calm weather? 14. Why is the ice filled with rock, gravel, and sand? This is a book that will intrigue and fascinate. It is like nothing you have ever encountered before!

IN the year 1947 Admiral Richard E. Byrd made a flight into the South Polar region of the world. Before he started on the venture, Byrd made a mysterious statement: "I'd like to see that land beyond the Pole. That area beyond the Pole in the center of the great unknown."

$21.95 + $5.00 S/H

TIMOTHY BECKLEY · BOX 753
NEW BRUNSWICK NJ 08903
mrufo8@hotmail.com

WANT TO LEARN MORE?
2 Disc DVD set Flying Saucers Come From Beneath The Earth, And Other Inner Earth Mysteries.
One critic proclaims: "Hollow Earth Lecture, Arctic Documentary and Sci Fi Movie...interesting combination."
Add $20 to order.

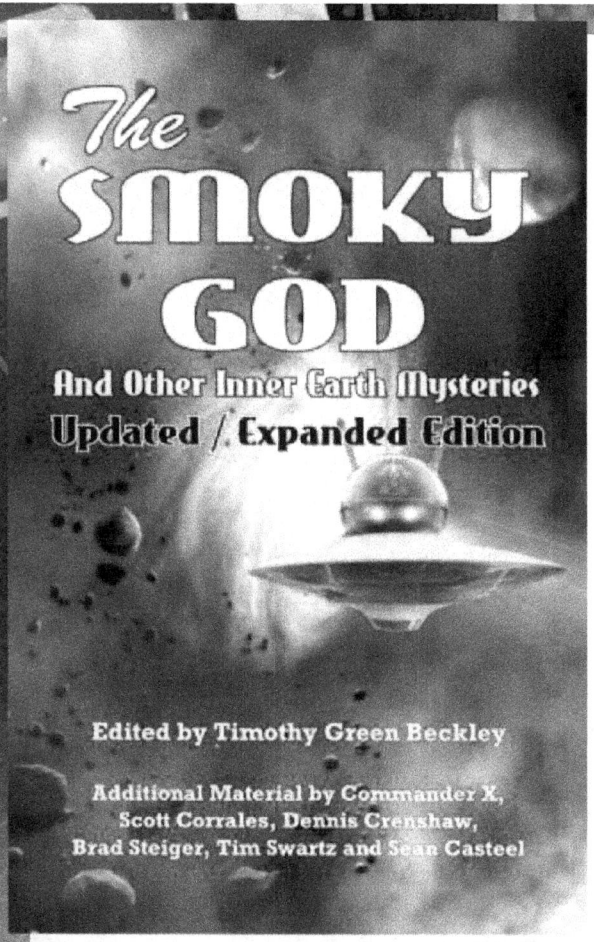

REVELATIONS ABOUT A BLOCKBUSTER DISCOVERY –

SCIENCE BE DAMNED! OUR PLANET IS HOLLOW AND LIFE EXISTS AT THE EARTH'S CENTER AND THROUGHOUT A VAST TUNNEL SYSTEM.

THE INTERIOR OF THE EARTH IS NOT MADE UP OF MOLTEN LAVA, BUT HOUSES A VAST CIVILIZATION UNHEARD OF BY THOSE LIVING ON THE PLANET'S OUTER SURFACE.

A rare, but all-too-true book, THE SMOKY GOD, tells of a fantastic journey made inside the Earth where the author meets a race of giants who befriend him. This valuable manuscript was believed to be lost for all time but is now available in its entirety, along with other incredible material that provides important evidence that our Earth is hollow and populated by a super race believed to be related to those who once resided on the continents of Lemuria and Atlantis.

Also included in this monumental work:

** The first interview ever with the princess of the underground city beneath Mount Shasta. ** A full description of the Agharta Network, its major cities, language, government, transportation, financial system, childbirth, age and Ascension. ** Underground locations of alien and Atlantean encampments and the existence of motherships and crystals the size of a New York City skyscraper.

* A fully-ordained minister's examination of Biblical references to the inner earth and its population of ten million, as well as the story of an ongoing war between inner earth and outer space people. ** An assessment of what one government official calls a "foreign military incursion" of British and American agents who show an inordinate interest in subterranean tunnels in which paranormal and "unusual" events have been known to transpire on a regular basis. ** How the discovery of one South American tunnel system caused this national government to declare that this discovery "may change our perspective of history!" ** Revelations regarding the existence of ancient mind reading "telog" devices that can scan your home and your brain, as well as other technologically advanced devices that go back thousand and thousands of years but which still exist underground.

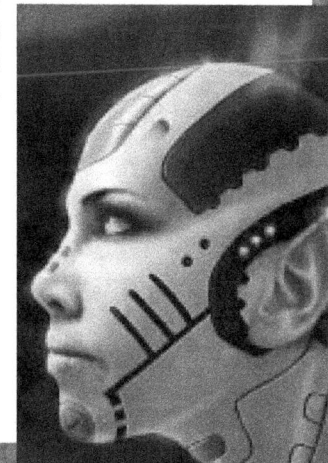

VENTURE TO AN UNSEEN WORLD TIME HAS FORGOTTEN! THIS IS THE MOST CENSORED BREAKTHROUGH NEWS OF ALL TIME!

Order THE SMOKY GOD EXPANDED EDITION

(NOW OVER 350 PAGES!) $20.00 + $5.00 S/H From

Timothy Beckley • Box 753 • New Brunswick, NJ 08903

TOUR GUIDE TO THE SPOOKIEST PLACES ON EARTH
JOIN A JOURNEY TO A LAND OF MYSTERY AND MYSTICISM ON THE EDGE OF REALITY
HERE ARE STRANGE TALES OF WITCHCRAFT, SPIRITUALISM, LOST RACES AND RELIGIOUS MIRACLES

South American folklore has its share of unique and fantastic myths and legends. There are incredible tales of magicians and their weird magical arts, strange creatures, ghosts and other unexplained mysteries. The first explorers that entered Latin America were dazzled by the endless tropical rainforests, the strange and diverse wildlife, and the indigenous peoples and their mysterious ways. Even today, South America, offers unique perspectives and influences on the paranormal that can not be found anywhere else on the planet.

Editor, writer, researcher, travel specialist and producer, John Wilcock has circled the world in search of the strange and unusual. He has also been editor of the Witches Almanac and is the co-founder of the Village Voice and Andy Warhol's Interview.

Wilcock states: — "The people of South America live in a world steeped in ancient traditions that enhance their lives with a rich taperstry of mystical beliefs. In modern Latin America, Catholicism is the predominate religion. However, especially in Brazil, Spiritism has become extremely prevalent, believing in the survival of the human personality and the possibility of communication with the spirit world."

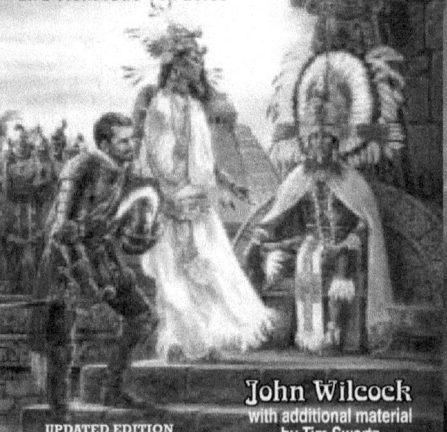

This Guide includes sections on ...—**The Dead Are Alive — **Spiritism In Brazil — ** Demons And Sinister Spirits —**Creatures From Out of This World —**Living Dinosaurs — **Here There Be Giants, etc.

Nearly 250 Large Format Pages – Send $20+ $5 S/H for AN OCCULT GUIDE TO SOUTH AMERICA.

THESE 'SPOOKY' TRAVEL GUIDES ALSO AVAILABLE

( ) <u>SECRETS OF DEATH VALLEY – MYSTERIES AND HAUNTS OF THE MOJAVE DESERT</u> – Includes the full text of George Van Tassel's *I Rode In A Flying Saucer*. Tales of Abandoned Mines, Mysterious Creatures, Deranged Killers, Spook Lights, Albino Bigfoot, Haunted Opera House. — $22.00

( ) <u>LOST WORLDS AND UNDERGROUND MYSTERIES OF THE FAR EAST</u> – Lost Cities and Civilizations. The Serpent Race. Shape Shifters of the Jungle. Forbidden Magick of Ancient Secret Societies. — $22.00

( ) <u>The Magick And Mysteries Of Mexico: Arcane Secrets and Occult Lore of the Ancient Mexicans and Maya</u> – Authored by Lewis Spence and Dragonstar. All that is known regarding the arcane knowledge and occult lore of the ancient Mexican peoples and their neighbors, the Maya of Central America and the Yucatan. It is the product of more than 35 years of research into the Pure Magic, Astrology, Witchcraft, Demonology and Symbolism practiced south of the border. — $20.00

( ) <u>Kahuna Power: Authentic Chants, Prayers and Legends of the Mystical Hawaiians.</u> Explore with Tim Beckley the most sacred knowledge of the Islanders, including a way to raise the dead. - $22.00

( ) SUPER SPECIAL – ALL FIVE "TOUR GUIDE BOOKS" AS LISTED JUST $75.00 + 8 S/H
From – TIMOTHY BECKLEY · BOX 753 · NEW BRUNSWICK, NJ 08903

www.ingramcontent.com/pod-product-compliance
Lightning Source LLC
Chambersburg PA
CBHW081323040426
42453CB00013B/2286